Essentials of English Grammar

THIRD EDITION

(The QUICK GUIDE to GOOD ENGLISH)

L. Sue Baugh

McGraw·Hill

New York   Chicago   San Francisco   Lisbon   London   Madrid   Mexico City
Milan   New Delhi   San Juan   Seoul   Singapore   Sydney   Toronto

Library of Congress Cataloging-in-Publication Data

Baugh, L. Sue.
    Essentials of English grammar : the quick guide to good English / L. Sue
Baugh.—3rd ed.
        p.   cm.
    Includes index.
    ISBN 0-07-145708-9 (alk. paper)
        1. English language—Grammar—Handbooks, manuals, etc.   2. English
language—Textbooks for foreign speakers.   I. Title.

PE1112.B33   2005
28.2′4—dc24   2005041535

9 10 11 12 13 14   DOC/DOC   1 4 3 2 1 0

ISBN 0-07-145708-9

Interior design by Nick Panos

McGraw-Hill books are available at special quantity discounts to use as premiums and
sales promotions, or for use in corporate training programs. For more information, please
write to the Director of Special Sales, Professional Publishing, McGraw-Hill, Two Penn
Plaza, New York, NY 10121-2298. Or contact your local bookstore.

This book is printed on acid-free paper.

Contents

Preface

Essentials of English Grammar is a concise guide to the basic rules of English grammar, usage, and style. It is designed to serve as a handy reference both to people who have only an occasional language question and to people who are developing the use of English as another language. It offers quick and convenient guidance to the fundamentals of the English language.

Essentials of English Grammar is arranged into two main parts. Part I, "Essentials of Grammar," covers the fundamental rules and exceptions for parts of speech, punctuation, sentence construction and patterns, capitalization, abbreviations, numbers, spelling, and word division. Part II, "Style Considerations," includes guidance on writing and combining sentences, brevity, clarity, accuracy, and gender-inclusive language. The appendixes offer additional resource materials.

Part I: Essentials of Grammar

Chapter 1, "Parts of Speech," emphasizes the building blocks of language and their grammatical functions. Examples show proper usage of each part of speech as well as common grammatical errors to avoid. This chapter gives special attention to verb forms and tenses, a subject that is often confusing. The six basic tenses used in English are discussed, accompanied by a complete conjugation of a regular verb.

Chapter 2, "Punctuation and Punctuation Style," discusses how to punctuate sentences for clarity and meaning. Specific guidelines show the proper usage of each punctuation mark in a variety of situations.

Chapter 3, "Sentences and Sentence Patterns," describes the components that make up the English sentence and the four sentence patterns that can be used to add variety and liveliness to writing. This chapter should be particularly helpful to those who wish to develop a more expressive style.

Chapter 4, "Capitalization, Abbreviations, and Numbers," is a thorough coverage of these three subjects, including attention to scientific and scholarly terms not ordinarily included in a brief reference text.

Chapter 5, "Spelling and Word Division," addresses another topic that baffles many writers—how to spell and divide words correctly when English seems a maze of exceptions to the rules. Spelling and word division guidelines are arranged into clear, simple rules and are accompanied by examples. A special feature of this chapter is an abundant listing of common prefixes and suffixes used in English, including their origins, meanings, and proper spellings when joined to root words.

Part II: Style Considerations

Chapter 6, "Sentences," contains guidelines on how to compose and combine clear, interesting, and varied sentences.

Chapter 7, "Brevity," includes rules for the elimination of wordy and redundant language.

Chapter 8, "Clarity," presents guidelines to support the choice of the best words to convey meaning. It focuses on the use of specific language, parallel structures, and correct references and on eliminating or reducing jargon.

Chapter 9, "Accuracy," offers suggestions to help writers check facts and other details in their writing to ensure accurate communication.

Chapter 10, "Gender-Inclusive Language," offers guidelines for use of nonsexist terms, social titles, salutations, and occupational titles.

End Matter

Four appendixes are included for the writer's convenience:

- Appendix A presents a list of the principal parts of the most commonly used irregular verbs.

- Appendix B clarifies many verb-preposition combinations.

- Appendix C provides a list of commonly confused words that sound similar but have different meanings.

- Appendix D is a list of commonly misspelled words, presented in the correct form.

For ease of reference, *Essentials of English Grammar* includes a detailed table of contents, a glossary, and a carefully constructed index.

Acknowledgments

I would like to thank the following people for their valuable assistance in the development of this book. Barrett Anders, Woodlands Academy of the Sacred Heart, and Dr. Robert Hausman, University of Montana, reviewed the manuscript and made many suggestions that improved the text. A special thanks to the editors at McGraw-Hill Trade for their help in developing the outline and content of the book and for shepherding the project through production. I would also like to thank Vilma Peña and Nicole Chaparro for their assistance in the preparation of this third edition.

PART I

Essentials of Grammar

Whether you're a native speaker of English or learning English as another language, grammar can be a confusing subject. The rules and guidelines in Part I will quickly and easily help you find what you need to know. In particular, the sections on verbs will help you learn how to use the often bewildering number of verb tenses in English.

Parts of Speech

Parts of speech are the basic building blocks of language. They include nouns, pronouns, verbs, adjectives, adverbs, prepositions, conjunctions, and interjections. In this chapter, each part of speech is defined, and its function in a sentence is discussed.

A good dictionary is an invaluable aid in understanding the pronunciation, grammatical function, spelling, and various meanings of different parts of speech. Figure 1.1 highlights the information that a dictionary offers.

An up-to-date dictionary should be part of any reference library. Consult it often for answers to questions about spelling, grammar, or usage.

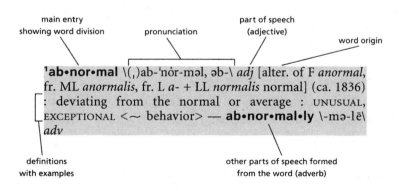

FIGURE 1.1 Sample Dictionary Entry

Nouns

A noun refers to a person, place, or thing (objects, concepts, ideas, or events).

Person	Place	Thing
ballplayer	stadium	glove
child	school	education
conductor	theater	performance
manager	company	excellence

Proper, Common, and Collective Nouns

Proper nouns are capitalized and name specific persons, places, or things. Common nouns identify general categories and are not capitalized, even when used with proper nouns (IBM machines, Minolta cameras). Collective nouns refer to a group of people, animals, objects, or other units.

Proper	Common	Collective
Texas A&M	university	trustees
Google	company	management
Julia Roberts	woman	movie cast
Nemo	fish	school
U.S.S. *Enterprise*	ship	fleet

Functions of Nouns

Nouns can be used as the subject, direct object, and indirect object of a verb; as the object of a preposition; and as an adverb or adjective. Nouns can also show possession.

Subject:	The **mail carrier** always rings twice.
	Violets are spring flowers. (tells *who* or *what* does or is something)
Direct object:	I finally sold my **car**. (tells *what* is sold)
Indirect object:	Harold fed the **cat** another olive. (tells *to whom* he fed the olive)

Object of preposition:	She gave directions over the **phone**. (tells *what* is the object of the preposition *over*)
Adverb:	The train leaves **today**. (tells *when*)
Adjective:	The **office** building faces the mall. (tells *what kind*, *which one*)
Possession:	The **parrot's** cage needs cleaning. My **father's** brother is my uncle. (shows *ownership* or *relationship*)

Plural Nouns

Most nouns can be made plural by adding *s* to the singular form. For other plural forms such as *es* and *ies*, see the section on Plurals on page 126.

Singular	Plural
highway	highways
bagel	bagels
base	bases

Collective Nouns. Collective nouns can be singular or plural depending on how they are used. When the group acts as a unit, the noun is considered singular. When the group acts as individual members, the noun is plural.

Singular:	The **management agrees** with the new president.
Plural:	The **management have** expressed different views.
Singular:	The **family is** celebrating three birthdays this month.
Plural:	The **family are** taking separate vacations.

For a more complete treatment of plural nouns, including compound and hyphenated nouns, see the section on Plurals on page 126.

Possessive Nouns

Possessive nouns are used to indicate ownership or relationship.

Singular Possessive. To form the possessive of singular nouns, add 's to all nouns. (For a complete discussion of the apostrophe used to indicate possession, see page 57.)

Singular	Singular Possessive
boy	the boy's iPod
hurricane	the hurricane's path

Plural Possessive. To form the possessive of a plural noun that ends in *s* or *es*, add an apostrophe to the end of the word.

Plural	Plural Possessive
sons	my sons' children
ships	the ships' escorts

For nouns that form the plural any other way, add 's to the end of the word.

Plural	Plural Possessive
children	children's toys
women	women's shoes
men	men's suits

Singular or Plural? To decide whether to place the apostrophe before or after the *s*, follow this simple rule: rephrase the sentence substituting an *of phrase* for the possessive noun to determine if the noun is singular or plural.

The (team's, teams') colors were on display.

Of Phrase	Possessive Form
colors of the team (singular)	team's colors
colors of the teams (plural)	teams' colors

Individual and Joint Ownership. To show individual ownership, make both nouns in the sentence possessive. To show joint ownership, make only the *final* noun possessive.

Individual ownership:	Mark's and Arlene's cell phones were stolen. (Each person had a cell phone that was stolen.)
Joint ownership:	Mark and Arlene's cell phone was stolen. (The cell phone belonged to both Mark and Arlene.)

In individual ownership, the noun following the possessive is generally plural (cell phones). In joint ownership, the noun is usually singular (cell phone). Look for this clue when deciding whether to use joint or individual possessive forms.

Pronouns

Pronouns take the place of one or more nouns or a group of words in a sentence. Like nouns, they can be used to refer to a person, place, or thing.

> The coach described several key plays. **He** wanted the team to memorize **them**. (*He* replaces *coach*; *them* replaces *several key plays*.)
> My car, which is in the garage, is getting too old for these winters. I should sell **it**. (*It* replaces *my car, which is in the garage*.)

The word or phrase that the pronoun replaces is called the *antecedent* of the pronoun. In the previous sentences, *coach* is the antecedent of *he*, while *my car, which is in the garage*, is the antecedent of *it*. (See more about antecedents on page 11.)

Pronouns are classified as *personal, intensive/reflexive, indefinite, possessive, relative, interrogative,* and *demonstrative.*

Personal Pronouns

Personal pronouns can be used in a variety of ways. They serve as the subject of a sentence, as the object of a verb or preposition, to show possession, to provide emphasis (called *intensive* pronouns), or to refer action back to the subject (called *reflexive* pronouns).

Subject:	**She** is simply too good to be true.
Object:	Tell **him** the parakeet died. (object of verb)
	Break the news to **him** gently. (object of a preposition)
Possessive:	**Your** hands are warm. Where did **my** glasses go?
Intensive:	The quarterback **himself** changed the call. (The pronoun *himself* emphasizes the subject *quarterback*.)
Reflexive:	Jane taught **herself** to use the scanner. We made the reservations **ourselves**. (The pronouns *herself* and *ourselves* refer the action back to the subjects.)

Case of Personal Pronouns

Personal pronouns have three cases: nominative (subject), possessive, and objective (object of verb or preposition). The following table shows the personal pronouns in all their case forms—including the intensive/reflexive forms—for the first person (*I, we*), second person (*you*), and third person (*he, she, it, they*).

Person	Case	Singular	Plural
First	nominative	I	we
	possessive	my/mine	our/ours
	objective	me	us
	intensive/reflexive	myself	ourselves
Second	nominative	you	you
	possessive	your/yours	your/yours
	objective	you	you
	intensive/reflexive	yourself	yourselves
Third	nominative	he/she/it	they
	possessive	his/her, hers/its	their/theirs
	objective	him/her/it	them
	intensive/reflexive	himself/herself/itself	themselves

Indefinite Pronouns

Indefinite pronouns refer to unspecified people or things. Many indefinite pronouns express some idea of quantity: *all, several, few, none*. Following is a list of the most commonly used indefinite pronouns.

all	each	most	other
another	either	neither	several
any	everybody	nobody	some
anybody	everyone	none	somebody
anyone	few	no one	someone
both	many	one	such

The board of directors needed a new president for the company. They appointed **someone** from outside the firm. (*Someone* replaces *new president.*)

Do you have any fantasy novels in your library? Yes, we have a **few**. (*Few* replaces *fantasy novels.*)

Possessive Pronouns

Possessive pronouns, unlike possessive nouns, never take an apostrophe. As shown in the table on page 8, the possessive forms are *my/mine, our/ours, your/yours, his/her, hers/its, their/theirs*. The pronoun *who* also has a possessive form, *whose*.

Whose gym shoes are on the floor?
I thought **my** wallet was lost, but the one Jameel found was **mine**.
Our vacation starts next week.
Those four suitcases are **ours**.
How can we get **your** dog to obey?
Is this **yours**?
Jerry Seinfeld never seems to lose **his** timing.
You have to take either **her** car or **theirs**. **Hers** is better.
The lawyers knew **their** client was probably guilty.

Possessive Pronouns vs. Contractions. People often confuse possessive pronouns with pronoun-verb forms that sound exactly like them (*its/it's, whose/who's, your/you're, their/they're*). To keep the possessive forms straight, remember this easy rule: possessive pronouns never take an apostrophe.

Pronouns that do take an apostrophe are contractions formed by the pronoun and a verb (*it's* = *it is*; *they're* = *they are*).

its	The shuttle fired **its** engines. (possessive)
it's	**It's** (*it is*) an awesome sight. (contraction)
whose	**Whose** video game is this? (possessive)
who's	We need to know **who's** (*who is*) coming. (contraction)
	Who's (*who has*) been eating my fudge? (contraction)
your	Can I use **your** fax machine? (possessive)
you're	**You're** (*you are*) welcome to try it. (contraction)
their	The Jaguar is **their** best car. (possessive)
they're	**They're** (*they are*) the top racing team. (contraction)

Possessive Pronouns and Gerunds. Gerunds are verb forms ending in *ing* that are used as nouns. In the sentence *Skiing is a wonderful sport, skiing* is a gerund used as the subject. If a pronoun precedes the gerund, the pronoun is generally in the possessive form.

Bill told me about **his snowboarding** down a mountainside.
She liked **my calling** her before I came over.
Her winning the lottery stunned us all.

The exception to this rule occurs when the pronoun follows verbs such as *see, hear,* and *watch.* In that case, use the objective form of the pronoun.

We didn't see **him leaving** the house.
The whole neighborhood heard **us playing** Nirvana.

Relative Pronouns

Relative pronouns can be used to avoid repeating the noun within a sentence. They are particularly helpful when one clause is embedded in another, because they keep both clauses grammatical.

The relative pronouns *who, whom,* and *whose* refer to people and animals, while *which* and *of which* refer to things. *That* can refer to people or things.

This violin, **which** he learned to play as a child, is a valuable instrument. (Using *which* avoids repeating the noun—*This violin, the violin he learned to play.*)

The woman **who** bought the suit returned it the next day. (*The woman she* would be ungrammatical.)

Interrogative Pronouns

The interrogative pronouns *who, whom, whose, what,* and *which* introduce questions. *Who, whom,* and *whose* indicate that the question refers to a person or animal; *what* refers to an object, idea, or event; and *which* can indicate either a person or thing.

Who called last night?
What is your earliest memory?
You can have a latte or a café mocha. **Which** do you want?

Demonstrative Pronouns

Demonstrative pronouns generally indicate nearness to or distance from the speaker, either literally or symbolically. *This, these, that,* and *those* usually refer to a specific noun, pronoun, or clause. However, sometimes the reference is to a general class of people or objects rather than to a specific antecedent.

This is my driver's license, and **that** is my credit card. (The driver's license is closer at hand.)

I don't envy **those** stuck at the airport tonight. (*Those* has no specific antecedent but refers to a general class of people: anyone stuck at the airport.)

Pronoun-Antecedent Agreement

The antecedent, as mentioned previously, is the word or phrase to which a pronoun refers. Pronouns must agree with their antecedents in person, case, and number.

Agreement in Person

Incorrect: The designer should know Quark thoroughly. Otherwise, **you** will have trouble creating book pages. (The pronoun *you* is in the second person, while its antecedent *designer* is in the third person. Therefore the correct pronoun is the third person *he* or *she*.)

Correct: The designer should know Quark thoroughly. Otherwise, **he** or **she** will have trouble creating book pages.

Agreement in Case

Incorrect: Is that Shaneel and Donna over there? Yes, it's **them.** (The objective case *them* is incorrect. The nominative case *they* is the correct form, even though it may sound strange to your ears.)

Correct: Is that Shaneel and Donna over there? Yes, it's **they.**

Agreement in Number

Incorrect: The data are obsolete and should be replaced. We can't use **it** any longer. (The plural noun *data* is the antecedent and requires the plural pronoun *them*.)

Correct: The data are obsolete and should be replaced. We can't use **them** any longer.

Imprecise Use of Pronouns. Pronouns should refer to a specific antecedent. Many writers misuse the pronouns *this, that, which, it*, and *they* by making them refer to entire sentences or ideas. Such errors can confuse the reader and must be avoided.

Vague: He wanted to raise the walls, put on the roof, and hang the doors all in one day. **This** was unrealistic. (The pronoun *this* refers to the sentence and not to any specific antecedent.)

Precise: His schedule was to raise the walls, put on the roof, and hang the doors all in one day. **This** was unrealistic. (The pronoun now refers to the antecedent *schedule*.)

Vague: The engineer asked for a meeting to discuss the new contract. I told her we couldn't do **that**. (The antecedent for the pronoun *that* is unclear. Is it the meeting or the discussion that the speaker is declining?)

Precise: The engineer asked if we could meet at her office. I told her we couldn't do **that**. (In this sentence *that* refers to the clause *meet at her office*.)

Double Antecedents. When *and* joins two antecedents, use a plural pronoun. If the antecedents are joined by *nor* or *or*, or when they form a unit (*ham and eggs*), use a singular pronoun.

An elm and a maple tree cast **their** shadows across the lawn.
Neither **Harriet nor Claire** has **her** keycard today.
Research and Development had **its** budget slashed this year.

Who *or* Whom?

The confusion over when to use *who* or *whom* has bothered writers for many years. In modern usage, the trend has been to drop the more formal-sounding *whom* and to use *who* in all cases. Following are the rules for using these two pronouns.

1. **Who** is used as the subject of a sentence or a clause (group of words containing a subject and verb) and never as an object.

   Who said we wouldn't make a profit? (*Who* is the subject of the sentence.)
   Can you tell **who** is talking right now? (*Who* is the subject of the clause.)
   The job goes to **whoever** answers the ad first. (*Whoever* is the subject of the clause.)

2. **Whom** is always used in the objective case as the object of a verb or preposition. It is never used as the subject.

Address the letter "To **Whom** It May Concern." (*Whom* is the
object of the preposition *to*.)

Whom did you see at the opera? (*Whom* is the object of the verb
see.)

Are there any singers **whom** you would recommend? (*You* is the
subject of the verb *recommend*; *whom* is the object of that verb.)

The job goes to **whomever** you call first. (*Whomever* is the object
of the verb *call*. *You* is the subject. Compare this sentence with
the one using *whoever*.)

Verbs

Verbs are words or groups of words that express action or a state of being
or condition. They provide the power or drive for sentences.

They **smashed** through the door. (action)
The ambassador **filed** a formal protest. (action)
Shawn **seems** unhappy today. (state of being)
The truck **looks** almost new. (condition)

Verbs that express a state of being or condition are called *linking verbs*.
These verbs link the subject with a noun, pronoun, or adjective that
describes or identifies it. The word or words linked to the subject are
referred to as a *subject complement*. In general, a verb is a linking verb if it
can be substituted for some form of the verb *seem*.

You **look** (*seem*) calm enough—are you?
She **felt** (*seemed*) ill at ease in the doctor's office.

The most common linking verb is *be* and its forms *am, is, are, was, were,
being*, and *been*. Other common linking verbs include the following.

Common Linking Verbs

appear	grow	remain	sound
become	hear	seem	stay
feel	look	smell	taste

Basic Verb Forms

A few verb forms are the basis for all verb tenses and phrases. These forms are as follows:

Base form:	Children **play** in the park.
Infinitive:	Tell them **to play** here.
Past tense:	They **played** all day yesterday.
Past participle:	He has **played** too long.
Present participle:	I am **playing** with her today.
Gerund (noun form):	**Playing** is children's "work."

Auxiliary Verbs

The past and present participles of the verb are also part of a word group that comprises a complete verb form: *has played, am playing*. The verbs used with these participles are called *auxiliary verbs* (also known as *helping verbs*). They signal a change in tense (*he walked, he has walked*) or a change in voice (*we told, we were told*). Following is a list of the most commonly used auxiliary verbs.

Auxiliary	**Auxiliary + Main Verb**
has/have	The jury **has rendered** a verdict.
	The defendants **have heard** the sentence.
is/are	The satellite **is boosting** the signal.
	They **are receiving** it in Hawaii.
can/could	He **can operate** in the morning.
	The patient **could come** home in a week.
should/would	The flight **should land** in New Jersey.
	We **would like** to arrive in New York.
do/did	I **do remember** you.
	We **did meet** last week.
will/shall	I **will tell** them to take the furniture away.
	Shall we **buy** the stuffed moose?
must/ought	They **must report** any suspicious activity.
	She **ought to call** the security guard.

Verb Tenses

Verb tenses allow us to talk about time, to place an action or state of being in the past, present, or future (*I called, I call/I am calling, I will call*). They also allow us to talk about intention, what would, could, or should be done (*I would have called, I can call, I will have called*).

Learning to use the right verb tense is important to convey intentions and the time of an action or state of being accurately and clearly. The various tenses in English are formed using the basic elements of the verb.

Base form:	march
Past tense:	marched
Present participle:	marching
Past participle:	marched
Auxiliary verbs:	am (was) marching, have (had) marched, will march

English has regular and irregular verbs. Learn the basic verb forms of these words to create the proper tenses and to avoid mixing tenses in writing.

Regular Verbs

Regular verbs follow the same pattern when moving from one tense to another. English has six basic tenses: *present, past, future, present perfect, past perfect,* and *future perfect*. In addition, the progressive and conditional forms are used for special functions. The *progressive form* (*I am singing, I was singing, I will be singing*) is used to indicate continuity of action rather than its completion. For example, compare *I wrote a letter* with *I was writing a letter*. The first sentence simply states that an action was completed in the past, while the second sentence implies that the action is connected to another event. Adverbs are often used with progressive forms to stress the continuous nature of the action or state of being (*He is **always** singing in the shower*). Progressive forms can be used with all six tenses. The *conditional form* (*I can sing, I could sing, I could have sung*) conveys intention to do or be something.

Following is a complete conjugation of the verb *to watch*. The function of each tense is discussed following the conjugation.

Present Tense

	Singular	Plural
First person:	I watch	we watch
Second person:	you watch	you watch
Third person:	he/she/it watches	they watch

Present progressive form: I am (you are) watching, etc.
Present conditional form: I can (I could) watch, etc.

Past Tense (Base Form of the Verb + *d* or *ed*)

	Singular	Plural
First person:	I watched	we watched
Second person:	you watched	you watched
Third person:	he/she/it watched	they watched

Past progressive form: I was watching, etc.
Past conditional form: I could have watched, etc.
   I could have been watching, etc.

Future Tense (*Will* or *Shall* + the Base Form of the Verb)

	Singular	Plural
First person:	I will (shall) watch	we will (shall) watch
Second person:	you will watch	you will watch
Third person:	he/she/it will watch	they will watch

Future progressive form: I will (shall) be watching, etc.

Present Perfect Tense (*Have* or *Has* + the Past Participle)

	Singular	Plural
First person:	I have watched	we have watched
Second person:	you have watched	you have watched
Third person:	he/she/it has watched	they have watched

Progressive form: I have been watching, etc.

Past Perfect Tense (*Had* + the Past Participle)

	Singular	Plural
First person:	I had watched	we had watched
Second person:	you had watched	you had watched
Third person:	he/she/it had watched	they had watched

Progressive form: I had been watching, etc.

Future Perfect Tense (*Will Have* or *Shall Have* + the Past Participle)

	Singular	Plural
First person:	I will (shall) have watched	we will (shall) have watched
Second person:	you will have watched	you will have watched
Third person:	he/she/it will have watched	they will have watched

Progressive form: I will have been watching, etc.

Functions of the Six Tenses

The six tenses show differences in the time of an action or a state of being, and using different tenses changes the meaning of a sentence.

Present Tense. The present tense is used to express an action or to state a fact that is occurring at the present time. The present tense also can be formed using auxiliary verbs for emphasis or to express intention.

I **live** here.
I **am living** here. (progressive)
I **do live** here. (emphatic)
I **can live** here. (conditional)

The present tense also is used to indicate habitual action or something that is true at all times.

She **goes** out every evening.

My grandfather believed that silence **is** (instead of *was*) golden.

Writers occasionally use the present tense when reviewing the contents of a book or describing past events to bring them vividly to life for the reader. This form of the present tense is known as the *literary* or *historical present*.

In his book on Alexander the Great, the Greek historian Arrian **dismisses** romantic legend and **concentrates** on sifting truth from fiction.

Past Tense. The past tense is used to express action or to help make a statement about something that occurred in the past and has not continued into the present.

I **lived** there.

I **was living** there while I was in school. (progressive)

I **did live** there. (emphatic)

Future Tense. The future tense is used to express an action or to help make a statement about something that will occur in the future.

I **will** (**shall**) live there.

I **will be living** there. (progressive)

I **am going to be living** there. (progressive)

I **can be living** there. (conditional)

The distinction between *will* and *shall* is no longer observed by most people. The two verbs can be used interchangeably for the simple future tense in the first person. However, in some cases, such as when asking for permission or consent, *shall* is the only form used.

Shall we go to the movie?

Shall I put the box here?

To use *will* in these sentences would change the meaning. However, except for such special uses, *will* and *shall* are equally correct.

> I *shall* call him.
> I *will* call him.

Perfect Tenses. Perfect tenses describe actions or states of being that happened at one time but are seen in relation to another time. For example, *I gave a donation to the Girl Scouts* is a simple statement about a past event and would be used to tell someone what happened in the past. *I have given a donation to the Girl Scouts* connects the past event to the present and can be used to imply a habitual or continuous action.

Present Perfect Tense. The present perfect tense is used to express an action or to help make a statement about something occurring at an indefinite time in the past or something that has occurred in the past and continues into the present.

> I **have lived** here for a long time.
> I **have lived** here for three months. (The speaker is still living there.)
> I **have been living** here for three months. (progressive)
> I **could have been living** here instead of where I am now.
>   (conditional)

Past Perfect Tense. The past perfect tense is used to express an action or to help make a statement about something completed in the past before some other past action or event.

> After I **had lived** here for three months, they raised the rent.
> After I **had been living** here for three months, they raised the rent.
>   (progressive)

Future Perfect Tense. The future perfect tense is used to express an action or to help make a statement about something that will be completed in the future before some other future action or event.

By this October, I **will have lived** here for six months.
By this October, I **will have been living** here for six months.
(progressive)

Irregular Verbs

Irregular verbs follow no fixed rules for forming the various past, present, and future tenses. You simply have to memorize them or consult your dictionary. Some of the most commonly used irregular verbs are listed in Appendix A. Here are a few examples of common irregular verbs that show the variety of their forms.

Base Form	Past Tense	Past Participle	Present Participle
be	was	been	being
break	broke	broken	breaking
fly	flew	flown	flying
lie (as in *recline*)	lay	lain	lying
ring	rang	rung	ringing

Common Errors in Using Verb Tenses

People often mix their tenses or use the wrong verb form when speaking. Although these errors may be overlooked in conversation, they are painfully evident in written communication. They often confuse the reader and affect the tone of the message. Study the following incorrect and correct sentences:

1. Use the correct verb form with each tense.

   Incorrect: He checked on the order and **has went** to pick it up.
   Correct: He checked on the order and **has gone** to pick it up.
   (*Gone* is the past participle of the verb *to go* and is the correct form to use with the auxiliary verb *has. Went* is the past tense form and is incorrect.)

Incorrect: I **done** the work last night and handed it in this morning.

Correct: I **did** the work last night and handed it in this morning. (*Done*, the past participle, is incorrect—the verb should be in the simple past tense *did*.)

Incorrect: Barb and Louise **have ordered** the tickets, **wrote** their friends about the concert, and **gave** away pictures of the band.

Correct: Barb and Louise **have ordered** the tickets, **written** their friends about the concert, and **given** away pictures of the band. (The auxiliary verb *have* requires the past participle for each verb in this sentence—*have ordered*, [*have*] *written*, [*have*] *given*. *Wrote* and *gave* are past tense forms of the verbs and are incorrect.)

Incorrect: The book **is** fascinating reading. It **provided** a detailed study of how cultures **were created**.

Correct: The book **is** fascinating reading. It **provides** a detailed study of how cultures **are created**. (The writer refers to the book in the present tense in the first sentence. All references that follow should also be in the literary or historical present tense.)

2. When describing two events in the past that did not occur at the same time, use the past perfect tense to refer to the event or action in the more distant past.

Incorrect: I suddenly **remembered** (past) that I **left** (more distant past) my purse at the office.

Correct: I suddenly **remembered** (past) that I **had left** (past perfect) my purse at the office. (Because leaving the purse at the office preceded remembering the fact, the past perfect form of *had left* should be used.)

Incorrect: Apartments **now existed** (past) where a city dump **was** (more distant past). (Using the past tense for both verbs suggests that the apartments and city dump are there together.)

Correct: Apartments **now existed** (past) where a city dump **had been** (past perfect). (The past perfect makes it clear that the city dump preceded the apartments.)

3. Do not use *would have* in "if clauses" that express the earlier of two past actions. Use the past perfect.

Incorrect: If he **would have thought** of it, he would have asked you to ride with us.

Correct: If he **had thought** of it, he would have asked you to ride with us.

Incorrect: If I **would have studied** harder, I'd have passed the course.

Correct: If I **had studied** harder, I'd have passed the course.

4. Use the present infinitive (*to play, to see*, etc.) to express action *following* another action.

Incorrect: I was disappointed because I had hoped **to have gone** with you. (Did the speaker hope *to have gone* or *to go*?)

Correct: I was disappointed because I had hoped **to go** with you. (The present infinitive *to go* is the correct form because the action it expresses follows the verb *had hoped*.)

Incorrect: She intended **to have visited** all her relatives. (Did she intend *to have visited* or *to visit*?)

Correct: She intended **to visit** all her relatives.

5. Use the perfect infinitive (*to have written, to have seen*, etc.) to express action before another action.

Correct: He was happy **to have seen** Ralph. (The speaker saw Ralph first; then he was happy about seeing him. Therefore the perfect infinitive *to have seen* is the proper form to use.)

6. In participial phrases, use *having* with the past participle to express action before another action.

Incorrect:	**Giving** my bike to Angela, I couldn't ride to the beach later that day. (The present participle *giving* is incorrectly used to express an action completed before the second action in the sentence.)
Correct:	**Having given** my bike to Angela, I couldn't ride to the beach later that day.
Incorrect:	**Painting** the front porch, he slept the rest of the day.
Correct:	**Having painted** the front porch, he slept the rest of the day. (He had to paint the porch before he could go to sleep. This could also be expressed by saying *After painting the front porch, he slept all day.*)

Mood

Verbs can be used to express differences in the intention or *mood* of the speaker or writer. There are three moods in English: indicative, imperative, and subjunctive. Each has a specific function.

The *indicative mood* is used when the speaker or writer wishes to make a statement or ask a question.

He **is leaving** tomorrow.
Does this plane **fly** to London?

The *imperative mood* is used for commands or requests.

Call Fredericks and **cancel** that shipment.
Please **return** the book to the library.
Turn right at the corner, and then **go** left.

The *subjunctive mood* uses a different form of the past and present to express matters of urgency, formality, possibility, or speculation.

Urgency:	I demanded that she **see** me immediately. (The indicative mood would use the form *sees* or *can see*—for example, I want to know if she *can see* me immediately.)
Formality:	He recommended that the zoning law **be** adopted. (The indicative mood would use *is adopted*—for example, the vote is 44 to 3; the law *is adopted*.)
Possibility:	If I **were** to sign the contract, we could not sell our own CDs. (The phrase *If I were to sign* expresses a future possibility. It has no reference to the past, even though *were* is a past tense verb form. Compare this sentence to *Because I signed the contract, we could not sell our own CDs*. In this sentence, the indicative mood describes an action that took place in the past.)
Speculation:	If he **were** king, he would make football the national pastime. (The subjunctive mood expresses something that is not true, a statement contrary to fact. The indicative mood, on the other hand, simply states a fact—for example, *If he was the king, then his brother was a prince*.)

Active and Passive Voices

If the subject of a sentence performs an action, the verb is in the *active voice*. If the subject receives the action, the verb is in the *passive voice*.

Active voice:	She **sold** a box of candy. (The subject *she* performs the action.)
Passive voice:	She **was sold** a box of candy. (The subject *she* receives the action.)
Active voice:	We **have delivered** the mail. (The subject *we* performs the action.)
Passive voice:	The mail **was delivered** by us. (*Mail* is now the subject and receives the action.)

The active voice adds interest and liveliness to a message. In general, use the active voice. Avoid weak and awkward passive verb constructions or long passages in which all the verbs are passive.

The passive voice, however, does have its contribution to make. It can be used to express an action in which the actor is unknown, when a more objective or diplomatic tone is required, or when it is desirable not to disclose the actor.

Active voice: Jim **locked** the front door before we left home.
Passive voice: The front door **had been locked** before we left home.
Active voice: Our sales manager **made** a mistake in completing your order.
Passive voice: A mistake **was made** in completing your order.
Active voice: We **have examined** your application and **must decline** your request for credit.
Passive voice: Your application **has been reviewed** and at this time your request for credit **must be declined**.

In the final example, the passive voice emphasizes the recipient of the action and minimizes the writer's role. Using the passive voice can make the decision seem less personally directed toward the reader. The speaker can then discuss the reasons for declining the application.

Subject-Verb Agreement

Just as pronouns must agree with their antecedents in person, case, and number, verbs also must agree with their subjects in person and in number.

The *first person subject* is the person or persons speaking in a sentence (*I, we*). The *second person subject* is the person or persons addressed (*you, you*). The *third person subject* refers to the person or thing spoken about and may be any noun or third-person pronoun (*he, she, it, they*).

Agreement in Person
First: **I am** hot. **We are** cold.
Second: **You look** fantastic.
Third: The **car rusts. She drives** fast. **They laugh** a lot.

Verbs must agree with their subjects in number. Therefore, a singular subject takes a singular verb; a plural subject takes a plural verb.

Agreement in Number

Singular	Plural
The **window is** open.	The **windows are** open.
She walks quickly.	**They walk** quickly.
I am going home.	**We are** going home.
You **can come** along.	All of you **can come** along.

Special Subject-Verb Agreement Cases

Compound subjects, collective nouns, and plural nouns used as titles of courses or subject areas can create confusion regarding subject-verb agreement. Following are guidelines for using a singular or plural verb in such cases.

Compound Subjects Joined by *and*—Singular Verb. Use the singular verb for compound subjects joined by *and* (1) when the subject is considered a unit (research and development) and (2) when both parts of the subject are modified by *each* or *every.*

> The **secretary and treasurer has** filed the minutes. (The secretary and treasurer is one person.)
> **Each** player and **every** team **receives** a prize for competing in the games.

Compound Subjects Joined by *and*—Plural Verb. Except for the cases already noted, compound subjects joined by *and* take a plural verb.

> **Rain and snow were** falling at the same time.
> **Tom and Samira have** resigned as coleaders.
> There **are one book and two paintings** on the floor.
> **Are the computer and the printer** compatible?

Compound Subjects Joined by *or* or *nor*—Singular Verb. Use the singular verb (1) if the subject next to the verb is considered singular or (2) if both parts of the subject are singular.

> The **drawers or the closet** is the place to look.
> **Is** the **cat** or the **ferret** in the garage?
> **Neither** Alan **nor** Julie **remembers** seeing my PalmPilot.

Compound Subjects Joined by *or* or *nor*—Plural Verb. The plural verb is used if the subject nearest the verb is plural or if both parts of the subject are plural.

> The **closet or the drawers are** the place to look.
> The **directors or the producers receive** all the credit.
> **Neither** the girls **nor** their teachers **were** aware of the approaching high tide.

Plural Nouns—Singular Verbs. Plural nouns used as the titles of courses or subject areas or as measurements or units of quantity (dollars, pounds, inches) take a singular verb.

> **Humanities has** a long reading list.
> I weighed myself, and **twelve pounds has** to go!
> **Five hundred miles seems** a long way to drive in one day.
> **Is $2,500** too much for this rug?

Collective Nouns—Singular or Plural Verbs. To emphasize the collective noun as a unit, use the singular verb. To refer to individuals within the group, use the plural verb.

> The **fleet sails** tomorrow at 4:30.
> The **Seventh Fleet have** three days to repair their vessels.
> Everyone knows how hard the **council works.**
> The **council are** divided about the tax-reform issue.
> When **is the team** going to play its next home game?
> The **team need** to recuperate from their injuries.

Prepositional Phrases and Other Matters Set Off from the Subject. Prepositional phrases following the subject or material set off from the subject by commas generally does not influence subject-verb agreement. To decide whether to use a singular or plural verb form, simply block out the prepositional phrase or additional material and look only at the subject and verb.

> **None** of the facts **has been proved** true. (*None* of the facts *has.*)
> **Any** of these students **writes** well. (*Any* [one] of these students *writes.*)
> Many **flowers**, such as the tulip, **grow** in northern climates. (Many *flowers*, such as the tulip, *grow.*)
> My **house**, unlike those houses, **looks** brand new. (My *house*, unlike those houses, *looks.*)

The exception to this rule occurs when the word *all* is followed by a singular or plural noun or pronoun. In this case, the prepositional phrase or material following *all* will determine whether to use a singular or plural verb.

> **All** of my apple pie **was eaten**. (Singular *pie* takes the singular verb *was eaten.*)
> **All** of my apple pies **were eaten**. (Plural *pies* take the plural verb *were eaten.*)

Adjectives

Adjectives modify nouns, pronouns, and other adjectives. They provide pertinent information about the words they modify by answering the questions *What kind? How many? Which one? How much?* Adjectives can add precision, color, and a dash of originality to writing.

> The zoo has a **two-year-old male** leopard. (What kind?)
> There may be **ten** planets in our solar system. (How many?)
> He gave her **that** hat over there. (Which one?)
> I have a **bigger** TV than he does. (How much?)

Demonstrative Adjectives

The demonstrative adjectives *which, what, this, these, that,* and *those* are used to emphasize which items are being singled out and their distance from the speaker. Unlike the pronoun forms of these words, demonstrative adjectives are never used alone.

> I feel sorry for **those** people caught in the flood. (Pronoun form: I feel sorry for *those* caught in the flood.)
> Take **this** car here and **that** car over by the driveway and park them both in the lot.
> I don't understand **which** person you're talking about.
> He doesn't know **what** schedule the driver is using this week.

Limiting Adjectives

Many adjectives are used to identify or number the nouns they modify. In nearly all cases, the limiting adjective comes before the noun. Following is a list of some of the more common of these adjectives.

Limiting Adjective	Noun
a/an	a mango, an orange
the	the hammer, the screwdrivers
few	few ideas
many	many calls
every	every week
each	each person
both	both lights
several	several cards
some	some cake
any	any window
most	most people
one	one country

Limiting adjectives *a, an,* and *the* are also known as *articles. A* and *an* are *indefinite articles* and refer to an unspecified item in a class (*a box, an apple*). *The* is a *definite article* and refers to one or more specific items in a class (*the box, the apples*).

Comparisons

Adjectives also are used to show comparisons between or among persons, places, or things. The positive, comparative, and superlative forms represent different degrees of a quality or characteristic.

The *positive* form is the base word (*low, cautious*). The *comparative* is formed by adding the suffix *er* or the word *more* (*lower, more cautious*). The *superlative* requires the suffix *est* or the word *most* (*lowest, most cautious*).

Positive	Comparative	Superlative
careful	more careful	most careful
incredible	more incredible	most incredible
proud	prouder	proudest
fast	faster	fastest
few	fewer	fewest

There are several irregular comparative forms as well.

bad	worse	worst
far	farther	farthest
good	better	best
less	lesser	least

When comparing two items, use the positive and comparative forms. For more than two items, use the superlative.

The black puppy is **smaller** than its brother. (comparative)
The brown puppy is the **smallest** of the eight. (superlative)
Jan has a **good** grade point average, Brian has a **better** one, while Joan has the **best** average of all. (positive, comparative, superlative)
That movie was **more** boring than a test pattern. (comparative)
He has the **most** expensive satellite dish on the block. (superlative)

Compound Adjectives

Compound adjectives generally are hyphenated when they precede the noun they modify. When they follow the noun, they are not hyphenated.

> She wanted a **blue-gray** living room.
> She even dyed the curtains **blue gray**.
> That is a **past-due** bill.
> The bill is **past due**.

Predicate Adjectives

When an adjective follows a linking verb such as *feel, become, seem, get, is, look,* and *smell,* the word complements the verb and is known as a *predicate adjective.* The adjective does not modify the verb but refers to the condition of the subject.

> She looks **beautiful**.
> He seems **unhappy**. Is he **all right**?
> The water is getting **hot**.

Adverbs

Adverbs modify verbs, adjectives, and other adverbs. They answer the questions *When? Where? How?* or *How much?* Adverbs describe an action or state of being in greater detail and can provide a more vivid picture of what is happening.

> She **always** signs her name with "Ms." (When?)
> They carried the chair **downstairs**. (Where?)
> Read it again **slowly**. (How?)
> He objected **strongly** to the judge's ruling. (How much?)

Forming Adverbs

Most adverbs end in *ly* and can be formed from the adjective. In some cases, however, the adjective and adverb both end in *ly*.

Noun	Adjective	Adverb
care	careful	carefully
collect	collective	collectively
coward	cowardly	cowardly
hour	hourly	hourly
thought	thoughtful	thoughtfully

Types of Adverbs

Adverbs indicating time, direction, place, or degree may look the same as nouns, prepositions, or adjectives. Following are examples of these types of adverbs, including some that end in *ly*.

Adverbs of Time/Frequency (When?)

always	frequently	occasionally
before	never	often
eventually	now	once
forever	Monday	seldom

Adverbs of Place/Direction (Where?)

across	in	there
around	out	through
backward	over	under
here	sideways	upstairs

Adverbs of Degree (How Much?)

completely	less	nearly
entirely	mildly	somewhat
excessively	most	thoroughly
however	much	

Adverbs of Manner (How?)

beautifully	equally	thankfully
carefully	handily	quickly
coldly	hotly	resentfully
earnestly	nicely	tirelessly

Comparisons

Adverbs—like adjectives—are used in comparisons. The *positive* is the base word (*fast, softly*). The *comparative* is formed by adding *er* or the word *more* (*faster, more softly*), and the *superlative* by adding *est* or the word *most* (*fastest, most softly*). A few adverbs have irregular forms (*well, better, best*).

He drives himself **hard**. (positive)
He drives himself **harder** than I think he should. (comparative)
He drives himself the **hardest** of anyone I know. (superlative)

I work **well** when I'm alone. (positive)
I work **better** when I'm with others. (comparative)
I work **best** late at night. (superlative)

The tiger moves **quietly** through the jungle. (positive)
The tiger moves **more quietly** than the deer. (comparative)
The tiger moves the **most quietly** of the three big cats. (superlative)

Adverb Position and Meaning

The position of the adverb can affect the meaning of the sentence. The most common error involves misplacing the adverb *only*. Make sure that the adverb position conveys what you intend to say.

Unclear:	We **only** walked to the store and not the bank. (Did the speakers only walk and not run? Or did they walk only to the store and not elsewhere? The meaning is unclear.)
Clear:	We walked **only** to the store and not to the bank.
Unclear:	She **frequently** calls the magazine editor. (Does she call the magazine editor more frequently than she calls anyone else? Or does she simply call the editor many times [frequently]?)
Clear:	She calls the magazine editor **frequently**.

In general, avoid splitting the verb phrase when using an adverb. While this rule is not carved in stone, it is a good one to keep in mind.

Avoid: I have **also** given the matter my attention.
Better: I **also** have given the matter my attention.
Avoid: He had **accurately** filled out the form.
Better: He had filled out the form **accurately**.

Adjective or Adverb?

Some words function as either adverbs or adjectives, and many writers may confuse them. Among the most troublesome words are *good, well, badly,* and *bad.*

    Good is an adjective and is always used as an adjective. Never use *good* to modify a verb.

You've done a **good** job. (modifies *job*)
I feel **good**. (predicate adjective referring to the condition of the
    subject)

Well is both an adjective, meaning in good health, and an adverb of manner, answering the question *how* something is done.

I feel **well**. (predicate adjective referring to the condition of the
    subject)
The reporter handled that story **well**. (modifies the verb *handled*)
She writes **well**. (modifies the verb *writes*)
("She writes **good**" is incorrect.)

The adverb *badly* is often mistaken for the adjective *bad*. *Badly*, an adverb of manner, indicates that something is done ineptly or poorly. It often follows an action verb.

He plays the piano **badly**. (modifies the verb *plays* and answers the
    question: *How does he play the piano? Badly.*)
They painted the room **badly**. (modifies the verb *painted* and answers
    the question: *How did they paint the room? Badly.*)

The adjective *bad* means "in poor spirits" or is used to describe the degree of something. When it follows a linking verb, it is a predicate adjective describing the condition of the subject.

She feels **bad**. (predicate adjective referring to the condition of the subject *she*)
That was a **bad** mistake. (adjective modifying *mistake*)

Never write *I feel badly* or *You look badly* when referring to the condition of the subject. These statements say that you feel (touch someone or something) poorly or that someone looks (sees things) poorly.

Prepositions

Prepositions are connecting words that show the relationship among words in a sentence. Nouns, pronouns, gerund phrases, or noun clauses can be the objects of prepositions. Together with the preposition they form a *prepositional phrase*. These phrases serve as adjectives modifying nouns and pronouns or as adverbs modifying verbs, adjectives, or other adverbs.

Put it **in** the box. (The noun *box* is the object of *in*; the prepositional phrase serves as an adverb and modifies the verb *put*.)
Give this to the usher **on** the right. (The noun *right* is the object of *on*; the phrase is used as an adjective, modifying the noun *usher*.)
After telling them a story, he put the children to bed. (The gerund phrase *telling them a story* is the object of the preposition *after*.)
Because of what they told us, we cut our trip short. (The noun clause *what they told us* is the object of the preposition *because of*.)

Following is a list of some of the most commonly used prepositions.

about	between	off
above	beyond	on
across	by	over
after	down	since
against	during	through

along	except	to
among	for	toward
around	from	under
at	in	until
before	inside	up
behind	into	upon
below	like	with
beneath	near	within
beside	of	without

Phrasal Prepositions

Although most prepositions are one word, some consist of phrases and are called *phrasal prepositions*. They are used frequently in spoken and written communication.

because of	in case of	instead of
by way of	on behalf of	on account of
in care of	in spite of	on the side of

In care of (c/o) is a common symbol used in correspondence. (*In care of* is a phrasal preposition that serves as the subject of the verb *is.*)

They traveled **by way of** Vermont. (The phrasal preposition *by way of* modifies the verb *traveled.* The noun *Vermont* is the object of the phrase.)

Common Errors to Avoid

Prepositions are among the most overworked words in the English language. Use the following guidelines to avoid committing two of the more common errors.

1. Avoid putting unnecessary prepositions at the end of sentences.

   Incorrect: Where are my keys **at**?
   Correct: Where are my keys?

Incorrect: Can I go **with**?
Correct: Can I go? Can I go **with you**?
Incorrect: Where did that remote get **to**?
Correct: Where is that remote?

2. In formal writing and business communications, avoid putting the preposition at the end of a sentence. Rewrite the sentence so that it has a correct prepositional phrase.

Avoid: They were not sure which college they should apply **to**.
Better: They were not sure **to** which college they should apply. (The preposition is now part of the phrase *to which college*.)
Avoid: Ask not whom the bell tolls **for**.
Better: Ask not **for** whom the bell tolls.

Prepositions Used with Verbs

These guidelines are not rigid. Winston Churchill once remarked, "This is the sort of English up with which I will not put."

Obviously, there will be exceptions to the rule, particularly when prepositions are used with verbs. In the quote by Churchill, the verb-preposition form is *to put up with*. In writing, however, it is best to recast the sentence to read "I will not put up with this sort of English."

Prepositions are used with verbs to change the meaning slightly or to distinguish between people and objects.

accompany by (a person)
accompany with (an object)
The president was **accompanied by** his wife.
The form was **accompanied with** a self-addressed, stamped envelope.

Knowing when to use the right preposition with a verb can be a challenge. Some of the most commonly confused verb-preposition combinations are listed in Appendix B at the end of this book.

Conjunctions

Conjunctions link words or groups of words to other parts of the sentence and show the relationship between them. The four basic conjunctions are coordinating conjunctions, correlative conjunctions, subordinating conjunctions, and linking adverbs.

Coordinating Conjunctions

Coordinating conjunctions *and, but, or,* and *nor* join two or more elements of equal rank. The conjunctions *but* and *nor* often are used with the adverbs *never* or *not*.

The elements joined by coordinating conjunctions can be single words—nouns, verbs, adjectives, adverbs, pronouns—or phrases or clauses. (Clauses are groups of words with a subject-verb combination such as *when she came to work* or *because they are sailing tomorrow.*)

> The telescope **and** its lens were repaired. (nouns)
> We called **and** called, but no one answered. (verbs)
> He is a sore **but** victorious player tonight. (adjectives)
> You can have it done quickly **or** thoroughly. (adverbs)
> She **and** I seldom agree on anything. (pronouns)
> We can go over the river **or** through the woods. (prepositional phrases)
> Did you know that he's **never** eaten a hot dog, had a real root beer, **nor** played miniature golf? (verb phrases)
> She went home last night **and** found the jury summons waiting for her. (clauses)

Correlative Conjunctions

Correlative conjunctions are coordinating conjunctions used in pairs, and they emphasize the elements being joined. Some of the most frequently used correlative conjunctions are as follows:

> both . . . and
> either . . . or

neither . . . nor
not only . . . but also

Correlative conjunctions also join elements of *equal rank*. Make sure that the elements following each part of the construction are truly equal.

E-mail **either** Judith **or** Andy about the party. (nouns)
It is **both** raining **and** snowing outside. (verb forms)
The trade talks were **neither** hostile **nor** overly friendly. (adjectives)
He **not only** installed a new DSL line **but also** added the latest CD
   burner. (verb phrases)

Subordinating Conjunctions

Unlike the conjunctions described in the preceding section, *subordinating conjunctions* join elements of *unequal rank* in a sentence. These elements are usually a subordinate clause (a group of words with a subject-verb combination that cannot stand alone) and an independent clause. Following is a list of commonly used subordinating conjunctions.

after	how	than	when
although	if	that	where
as	in order that	though	which
as much as	inasmuch as	unless	while
because	provided	until	who/whom
before	since	what	whoever/whomever

Subordinating conjunctions can be used to introduce a sentence as well as to join elements within it. When a subordinate clause comes at the beginning of a sentence, it is followed by a comma. No comma is used when the subordinate clause comes at the end of the sentence.

Before we left the theater, I had to dry my eyes.
I had to dry my eyes **before** we left the theater.
Provided the books arrive, we can start class Tuesday.
We can start class Tuesday **provided** the books arrive.

Restrictive and Nonrestrictive Clauses. Some clauses provide additional information about a person, place, or object within a sentence. When the clause is essential to the meaning of that sentence, it is known as a *restrictive clause*. When it is descriptive but not essential, it is called a *nonrestrictive clause*.

Restrictive:	The city **that was built along the river** escaped the fire. (The clause *that was built along the river* distinguishes this city from all others in the area. The information is essential to the sentence.)
Nonrestrictive:	The city, **which was built along the river**, escaped the fire. (In this sentence, the clause *which was built along the river* is simply descriptive information.)

Notice that the subordinating conjunction changes from *that* in a restrictive clause to *which* in a nonrestrictive clause. In general, *that* is used to indicate information essential to the meaning of the sentence. *Which* indicates information that is not essential.

To decide whether a clause is restrictive or nonrestrictive, eliminate the clause from the sentence and determine if doing so changes the meaning.

The accountant **who works for John** has been missing for three days.
The accountant, **who works for John**, has been missing for three days.

In the first sentence, *who works for John* identifies which accountant among several is missing. The second sentence implies that the *accountant*, as opposed to the receptionist or some other individual, has been missing. The information *who works for John* can be eliminated without changing the meaning of the sentence.

Linking Adverbs

Linking adverbs are used to join two *independent clauses*, that is, clauses with a subject-verb combination that can stand alone. Linking adverbs indicate the relationship between two ideas expressed in independent clauses. In general, linking adverbs reflect results, contrast, or continuation.

Results	Contrast	Continuation
accordingly	nevertheless	furthermore
as a result	however	further
therefore	nonetheless	in addition
thus	conversely	also

Linking adverbs can come at the beginning of the second clause they are joining. In such cases, they are usually preceded by a semicolon and followed by a comma. They also can stand within the second clause or sentence and often are set off by commas.

We arrived late at night; **however**, no one complained.

I fail to see your point; **furthermore**, your entire argument is off the subject.

The strike delayed shipment; **therefore**, your order will not be sent on the date we promised.

The train slipped off the track at Innsbruck; the passengers, **accordingly**, had to continue by taxis.

The storm ruined two speakers; the band, **however**, had spare ones in the van.

Interjections

Interjections are words used to express emotion or to catch the reader's attention. Interjections are rarely used in formal or business writing but do appear in advertising and promotional material, fiction, informal writing, and personal letters.

Common Interjections

These are some of the most commonly used interjections:

ah	hey	no way
alas	hooray	oh
congratulations	hurry	ouch
good grief	my goodness	outstanding
great	never	ugh
help	no	wow

Punctuation

Strong interjections are punctuated with an exclamation point (*wow! ouch! hooray!*). The first word following the exclamation point is capitalized because it is the first word in a new sentence.

Milder interjections are set off by commas and often introduce a sentence (*indeed, yes, well*). The word following the comma is not capitalized because it is a continuation of the same sentence.

Strong interjections:	**Excellent!** That was a perfect dive.
	You may be saying, "**Hey!** Why is the coffee cold?"
Mild interjections:	**No,** we can't visit you this summer.
	Well, I just thought I'd ask.

Punctuation and Punctuation Style

Punctuation serves two important purposes in written communication. First, it helps present ideas clearly and accurately. It indicates where one thought ends and another begins, shows relationships among ideas, and separates items in a series. Second, punctuation is used in abbreviations and in figures expressing time, quantities, and measures.

This chapter covers proper usage of end marks, commas, semicolons, colons, quotation marks, apostrophes, hyphens, dashes, parentheses, brackets, and ellipses.

End Marks: Period, Question Mark, Exclamation Point

End marks usually come at the end of a sentence. However, they also can be used after single words or within a sentence.

Period

The *period* is used at the end of a complete sentence, which can be a statement, command, or request. It is a visual marker to the reader that one complete thought has ended and that another may follow. In informal writing, periods can be used with single words.

Statement:	You shouldn't drive and talk on the cell phone.
Request:	Please hang up and drive.
Command:	Get off the cell phone and drive.
Single words:	Thanks. I feel much safer.

Periods are also used in many abbreviations. For a more complete discussion of abbreviations, see pages 86-100.

Saint	St.
Avenue	Ave.
American Bar Association	A.B.A.

Question Mark

A *question mark* is used at the end of a sentence that asks a direct question. It is not used at the end of a statement that contains an *indirect* question. In informal writing, question marks also can be used with single words.

Direct question:	Are you going to the preview tonight?
Indirect question:	I asked them if they were going to the preview tonight.
Single words:	What? I couldn't hear you over the TV.
	So? It's no trouble to feed one more person.

Polite Requests. Many business letters contain requests for information, compliance, reply, or permission. These requests can be punctuated using either a period or a question mark.

Period:	Would you please send me your company's website address.
Question mark:	Would you please send me your company's website address?

Series of Questions. Question marks are used after each question in a sentence containing a series of questions.

How much are you willing to gamble on your future? your family's
   health? your career?

Quotation Marks. Question marks are placed *inside* quotation marks
when the quoted material is a question. Otherwise, they are placed *outside*
quotation marks.

"Are the sets ready?" the director asked.
I just finished the short story "Where Is Paradise?"
Have you read "The Scarlet Ibis"? (The quoted material is not a
   question. The entire sentence is the question.)
Did he say "no vacation" or "no early vacation"?

Exclamation Point

Exclamation points add emphasis to sentences, phrases, or single words.
They are like a red flag waved at the reader and as such should be used spar-
ingly. Exclamation points are a familiar sight in advertising and promotional material.

Wait! Don't touch that wire!
I can't believe she said that!
Don't delay! Order your DVDs now!

Comma

The *comma* is the most commonly used and abused punctuation mark.
People often insert commas between subject and verb or when they reach
the end of a thought, without regard for the rules of comma usage.

Commas are used to separate words or groups of words in a list or parallel construction; to set off introductory elements, interruptions, and
words moved from their usual position; and to coordinate such grammatical structures as compound predicates, coordinate adjectives, and descriptive appositives and modifiers. On the other hand, some comma uses have
little to do with the meaning of a sentence and are inserted to prevent mis-

reading or to create emphasis. In a few cases, they simply represent traditional ways of punctuating various grammatical elements.

This section discusses some of the more common uses and abuses of this often troublesome punctuation mark.

Series Comma

Commas separate items in a series. The items can be single words, phrases, or clauses. Although current practice allows the final comma to be dropped before the final conjunction (*or, but, nor,* and *and*), including the comma can avoid possible confusion for the reader.

> We brought sandwiches, wine, cold soup, and chocolate cake on the picnic.
> The conductor set up his stand, took out the score, and lifted his baton. (verb phrases)
> She is vice president of operations, sales and resources and personnel. (Are the final categories *sales and resources,* and *personnel* or are they *sales,* and *resources and personnel?* A final comma would make the categories clear.)

Independent Clauses

When two independent clauses are joined by *and, but, or, nor,* or *for,* use a comma before the conjunction. However, no comma is needed if the clauses are very short.

> Her gymnastics routine was brilliant, and the judges gave her a 99.46.
> Yolanda knew we'd be late, but she left anyway.
> He can play the guitar, or he can do his magic show.
> Stir the batter and add the eggs slowly.
> They came early and they stayed late.

A comma is not used when *and, but, for, or,* or *nor* joins two verbs that share the same subject.

Kerry Wood **pitches** with the best of them and **bats** better than most outfielders.

Shelly **has never cooked** a meal nor **washed** her own clothes.

Introductory Clauses, Phrases, Expressions

Use a comma after introductory phrases or clauses unless they are very short. When expressions such as *no, yes, in addition, well,* and *thus* begin a sentence, they are followed by a comma.

When Ansel Adams took a photograph, he knew exactly what would appear in the picture.

Speaking of food, isn't anybody hungry?

In summer we always try to get outside more. (Short phrase *in summer* does not require a comma.)

Well, losing one game doesn't ruin an entire season.

Thus, I feel your qualifications make you perfectly suited for this job.

Nonrestrictive Clauses and Nonessential Material

Commas set off nonrestrictive clauses and expressions that interrupt the sentence or that add incidental information or description.

The rodeo, always held in August, draws tourists from all over.
(*Always held in August* is a nonrestrictive clause.)

We wanted to finish, of course, but didn't know how.

The new officer, I'm sure you remember him, locked himself out of his car.

Direct Address

Words used in direct address are set off by commas regardless of their position in the sentence.

Greg, can you fix my e-mail?
They heard about the trouble, Jean, and wanted to help.
Please sign this receipt, Ms. Liang.

Commas and Clarity

At times commas are used to avoid confusing the reader when a sentence can be read in more than one way.

In autumn nights grow steadily longer. (On first reading, *autumn* and *nights* appear to go together. It's evident from the rest of the sentence, however, that they are separate. A comma after *autumn* would make the meaning clear immediately.)
In autumn, nights grow steadily longer.

Traditional Comma Uses

Commas are used in certain conventional situations including dates, addresses, the salutations and closings of informal letters, and certain forms of proper names or names followed by a title.

We were married June 22, 1941, in Los Angeles. (When only the day and month are used, no commas are necessary. *We were married on June 22 in Los Angeles.*)
Send your rebate coupon to Harvard House, Suite 2920, 467 West Rhine Street, Portland, Oregon.
Dear Harriet,
Sincerely yours,
Truly yours,
Samuel Stanislaw, Jr. (but *Samuel Stanislaw III*)
Judith Gallagher, PhD
Linda Marks, director

Comma Faults

Many people use commas incorrectly. The following guidelines point out common errors in style.

1. Never use commas to separate subject and verb.

   Incorrect: Finding a lead singer for the band, has been an ordeal. (The noun phrase *Finding a lead singer for the band* is the subject and should not be separated from the verb *has been*.)

   Correct: Finding a lead singer for the band has been an ordeal.

2. Never use commas to separate two phrases or subordinate clauses joined by a conjunction.

   Incorrect: The waiter suggested that we order a white wine, and that we try the Cajun appetizers.

   Correct: The waiter suggested that we order a white wine and that we try the Cajun appetizers.

   Incorrect: Ming-Jie painted her room, but not the hallway.

   Correct: Ming-Jie painted her room but not the hallway.

   Incorrect: After the treaty was signed, both sides pulled back their troops, and reduced their armored divisions.

   Correct: After the treaty was signed, both sides pulled back their troops and reduced their armored divisions.

3. In a series, never use a comma to separate a modifier from the word it modifies.

   Incorrect: They drove through a damp, cold, eerie, fog.

   Correct: They drove through a damp, cold, eerie fog.

   Incorrect: That is a ridiculous, immature, wicked, suggestion.

   Correct: That is a ridiculous, immature, wicked suggestion.

Semicolon

A *semicolon* represents a stronger break than a comma but not as complete a stop as a period or colon. Semicolons are used to separate independent clauses in a variety of special circumstances. They also serve to group items in a series when the items contain internal punctuation.

Independent Clauses

Use a semicolon to join two independent clauses that are similar in thought but are *not* joined by the coordinating conjunctions *and, but, or, nor, for,* or *yet.*

The house stood empty for years; no one would buy it.
The river raged through the gorge; her small tent was swept away in its path.

Joined by a Linking Adverb. When two independent clauses are joined by a linking adverb such as *accordingly, however, therefore,* or *thus,* use a semicolon at the end of the first clause. The linking adverb is usually followed by a comma or set off by commas if it falls within the second clause.

The turtle survived its two-story fall; however, it was never quite the same again.
The conference ended last Thursday; therefore, we can get back to business on Monday.
Margaret told me not to stay in a motel; she suggested, instead, that I stay at her house.

Clauses with Internal Punctuation. A semicolon may be used to separate two independent clauses if one or both of the clauses contain internal punctuation. The clauses may or may not be joined by conjunctions or linking adverbs.

She owns two dogs, a goat, and a llama; they stay outside all year.
Walter, the one with the allergies, read his story in class; and everyone thought it was excellent.
The dark, dusty street looked deserted; but I kept hearing footsteps behind me.

Series

Use semicolons to separate items in a series if the items contain internal punctuation.

> The speakers included Jeff Hines, vice president; Alberta Corazon, director of finances; Edward Singh, human resources; and Nancy Meripol, assistant to the president.
>
> We ordered five cartons of color-printer paper; six lined, medium-sized stationery pads; and nine boxes of assorted pens, pencils, and markers.

Colon

Colons represent a more complete break than semicolons but not as complete a stop as a period.

Before a Series or List

Colons are used to introduce a series or list only after a complete sentence. When the series immediately follows a verb or preposition, do not use a colon.

Incorrect:	Our five travel choices are: the Bahamas, Hawaii, Mexico City, Acapulco, and Peoria.
Correct:	We have five travel choices: the Bahamas, Hawaii, Mexico City, Acapulco, and Peoria.
Incorrect:	They were interested in: one brass bed, two lace pillows, one afghan comforter, and a chamber pot.
Correct:	They were interested in the following items: one brass bed, two lace pillows, one afghan comforter, and a chamber pot.

Between Independent Clauses

Use a colon to introduce a question or related statement following an independent clause. The second independent clause may or may not begin with a capital letter. Whichever way you choose, be consistent in your writing.

> She had only one thought: What was she going to do now?
> I know the answer: reverse the two equations.

Time

Colons are used to express time in figures. Do not use the words *o'clock* after the figures. However, expressions such as *noon, in the afternoon, AM, PM,* and *midnight* can be used.

10:30 AM	4:35 PM
12:00 midnight	8:30 in the morning

Formal and Business Communications

Colons follow the salutation in a formal or business letter, report, memo, or other type of business communication.

Dear Mr. Winfield:	To the Research Staff:
Dear Buyer:	To All Managers:
Dear President West:	Attention Union Members:

Quotation Marks

Quotation marks enclose a direct quotation, that is, the repetition of someone's exact words.

> "Keep your head down and charge!" the coach said.
> Her exact words were, "Bake the bread at 350 degrees."

Indirect quotations do not take quotation marks.

The coach said to keep your head down and charge.
She told us to bake the bread at 350 degrees.

Punctuation with Quotation Marks

Commas and periods are always placed *inside* the quotation marks even if the quoted material is contained within the sentence.

She thinks we're "off the wall," but I think our idea will work.
We've heard him say a thousand times, "Waste not, want not."
"Tell me something I'll remember forever," she said.
You've read the poem "Ash Wednesday," haven't you?

Semicolons and colons are always placed *outside* the quotation marks.

Look up the title under "Animated Cartoons"; copy the cartoon
   features listed there.
The following animals are considered "marsupials": kangaroo,
   wombat, koala.

Question marks and exclamation points are placed *inside* the quotation marks if they are part of the quoted material. Otherwise they are placed *outside* the quotation marks. Only one end mark is used at the end of a sentence containing quoted material.

Have you read the report "The Over-Scheduled Child"? (The entire
   sentence is the question; the end mark comes after the final
   quotation mark.)
He sent Irene the article "Why Can't Ivan Compute?" (The title is a
   question; the end mark comes before the final quotation mark.)
"Dinner is ready!" he called.
I can't believe they want us to increase sales "by 20 percent"!

Brief and Long Quotations

Quoted material that is only two or three lines long is enclosed in quotation marks and included as part of the regular text.

> The movie critic was blunt about her reactions to the film. She stated that it "has the intelligence of a jellyfish and as much reality as a *Survivor* series."

Longer quotations have no quotation marks and are set off from the rest of the text.

> The movie critic was blunt about her reactions to the film.
>> This movie should suffer an early and merciful death. It has the intelligence of a jellyfish and as much reality as a *Survivor* series. I don't know what the director intended for this film; but unless it was to bore us to death, he has certainly failed.

Single Quotation Marks

Single quotation marks are used to set off a quote within a quote.

> Carla said, "Every time I hear the song 'Into the West' I want to cry."
> "When I asked him what he needed, he replied, 'A passport.'"

Titles

Quotation marks are used to enclose the titles of articles, chapters of books, poems, reports, many governmental publications, short stories, individual songs, workshop or conference titles, and titles of proceedings.

> "Ballad of the Sad Cafe" is required reading in most college literature programs.
> The song "Somewhere over the Rainbow" was almost left out of the classic movie *The Wizard of Oz.*
> Read the chapter "How Diet Affects Immune Functions" before you change your eating habits too much.

The report "Equality in the Workplace: A Ten-Year Study" shows how much work still needs to be done.

Billy Collins' poem "Study in Orange and White" appears in one of his recent collections.

The IEEE international conference focused on the theme "Nanotechnology: Practical Applications."

Throughout the weekend, we will offer two workshops titled "Living with Stress" and "Getting Control of Your Finances."

Terms and Expressions

Use quotation marks to enclose terms and expressions that are considered odd or unusual (slang terms in a formal report) or that are likely to be unknown to the reader (jargon, technical terms).

The President told reporters he regarded his opponent as a "flip-flopper."

Not many people know the functions of "T cells" or "B cells" in the immune system.

Scott said he was as full as a "bug-eyed tick."

The term "blog" should be defined in your book.

Apostrophe

The *apostrophe* is used to show possession and to form the plural of many nouns and symbols, as well as to indicate the omission of letters in contractions. (Possessive nouns and pronouns are also covered in Chapter 1 under Nouns and under Pronouns.)

Possessive of Singular Nouns

The possessive of a singular noun is formed by adding 's. Names that end in a *z* sound often take only the apostrophe to avoid the awkwardness of too many *s* sounds.

the **mechanic's** wrench   **Gloria's** backpack
the **tree's** leaves   Mr. **Jones'** iPod
Moses' tablets   **Carlos's** notebook
Mrs. **Gonzales's** maid   Ned **Stanis's** boots

Possessive of Plural Nouns

The possessive of plural nouns ending in *s* is formed by adding only the apostrophe. All other plural nouns take *'s*.

the **Harlands'** trip   the **trees'** leaves
children's shoes   **men's** sports wear
the **teams'** scores   **women's** networks

Possessive of Indefinite and Personal Pronouns

Indefinite pronouns (*everyone, no one, anybody, everybody, someone, somebody, one*) require an apostrophe to form the possessive. However, personal possessive pronouns (*his, hers, theirs, your/yours, my/mine, our/ours*) do not use an apostrophe.

Is this **someone's** book?   Yes, the book is **hers**.
I'll take **anyone's** ideas. **Your** ideas are great.

Individual and Joint Possession

To show *joint possession* by two or more organizations, companies, or individuals, only the last word takes *'s* or an apostrophe. In cases of *individual possession*, both nouns and pronouns take *'s* or the apostrophe only.

Joint possession: **Lin and Chan's** bicycle (The bicycle is owned by both Lin and Chan.)
the **vice presidents'** office (The office is used by more than one vice president.)
IBM and Xerox's new venture (The two companies are working together on one venture.)

Individual possession: Lin's and Chan's bicycles (Notice the plural noun after the names—a clue that each person owns a bicycle.)
her **father-in-law's** and **brother's** golf scores
Texaco's and **BP's** annual reports

Units of Measure as Possessive Adjectives

Units of measure such as *day, week, yard, cent,* and *hour* take *'s* or an apostrophe when used as possessive adjectives.

a **moment's** peace	ten **minutes'** work
a **month's** pay	three **weeks'** pay
a **dollar's** worth	two **cents'** worth

Plural Forms of Symbols

The apostrophe or *'s* is used to form the plural of letters, numbers, signs, symbols, and words referred to as words.

All the **R's** in this article were printed backward.
Mark these items with **X's** and those with **O's**.
Your **3's** look like **8's**.
How many **and's** can you put in one sentence?
The printer smudged all the **g's** in my report.
We can use **+'s** and ***'s** in the chart.

Contractions

The apostrophe is also used to indicate letters that have been omitted to form contractions of verbs. Contractions are used in informal writing and conversation, but are generally avoided in formal writing.

She will come tomorrow.
She'll come tomorrow. (*wi* in *will* omitted)

I have not heard from him.
I've not heard from him. (*ha* in *have* omitted)

Formal writing: **Do not** send the second shipment by UPS.
Informal writing: **Don't** send the second shipment by UPS. (*o* in
                          not omitted)

Hyphen

Hyphens are used to join two or more words that are used as a single unit, to join continuous numbers, to connect some prefixes and suffixes with their nouns, to divide words at the end of a line, to link two last names, and to avoid confusing or awkward word constructions.

Compound Numbers and Fractions

Hyphens are used with compound numbers from twenty-one to ninety-nine and with fractions used as adjectives. However, when fractions serve as nouns, no hyphen is used.

twenty-one gun salute   a **two-thirds** majority
sixty-five and over   a glass **three-fifths** full (But do not
                                 hyphenate *three fifths* when used as a noun,
                                 such as *three fifths* of the voters.)

Continuous Numbers

Hyphens are used to link dates of birth and death, pages of material, scores of games, and other instances in which the relationship between the numbers needs to be shown.

Christoper Reeve, "Superman" (**1952-2004**)
Read pages **15-32** in your statistics book.
The Bears beat the Rams **21-0.**
All the children ages **8-12** are eligible for camp.

Prefixes and Suffixes

Prefixes *ex, self,* and *all* and the suffix *elect* always take a hyphen whether they are used as modifiers or as nouns. Hyphens also are used with all prefixes before proper nouns and adjectives.

self-esteem	secretary-elect	all-Canadian team
ex-director	all-encompassing	pro-French

Compound Adjectives

When compound adjectives are used before the noun, they are hyphenated. When they follow the noun, no hyphen is used. If one of the modifiers is an adverb ending in *ly*, do not use a hyphen in the compound adjective.

a **decision-making** process	a process for **decision making**
a **well-run** program	a program that is **well run**
a **city-owned** business	a business that is **city owned**
organically grown fruit	fruit that is **organically grown**
publicly owned parks	parks that are **publicly owned**

Word Division

Hyphens are used to divide words at the end of a line as a reminder that the rest of the word is to follow. Words cannot be divided arbitrarily but only between syllables. See the section on Word Division in Chapter 5 for rules on dividing words at the end of a line.

We were almost in Niles **Town-
ship** when our car broke down.
Sam didn't really want to **continue** the trip, but I did.

Hyphenated Names
Hyphens are used to join two last names.

Karen Norridge-Adams   Mr. Michael Harrington-Kelly
the Henderson-Smythes   Mr. and Mrs. Burns-Schroeder

To Avoid Confusion
Use hyphens to prevent confusion or awkwardness in sentences.

re-creation (prevents confusion with *recreation*)
anti-intellectual (avoids awkwardness of *antiintellectual*)
sub-subentry (avoids confusion of *subsubentry*)

Dash
A *dash* indicates a break in thought or the addition of information within a sentence or at its end. A dash is typed using two hyphens (although most word-processing programs can be set up to automatically insert a dash when you type two hyphens). There is no space before or after the punctuation mark.

The woman came running around the corner—I couldn't see her face—and disappeared down the alley.
This building—and every building on the street—will be torn down.
Marsha Nagib—you know her, I think—told me we might close early today.

A dash can be used to mean *namely, that is,* or *in other words* to introduce additional information or an explanation.

I thought about taking another route—the one through West Virginia.
There's only one way to win—don't play the game.

Parentheses

Parentheses enclose material that is an interruption of the text but adds information.

> The park (in Washington) is always crowded in summer.
> I know the answer (I think) to the final question.

If the material enclosed falls at the end of a sentence, the end mark is placed *outside* the closing parenthesis. If the material is a complete sentence within itself, the end mark is placed *inside* the closing parenthesis.

> We provide a complete list of stores (see our website).
> We provide a complete list of stores. (See our website.)

Brackets

Use *brackets* to enclose additions to quoted material. These additions, made by editors or writers, usually clarify or comment on the material.

> "Mark Twain said it [the river] taught him all he ever knew about life."
> "Virginia Woolf lived with him [Lytton Strachey] while recovering from her illness."
> "There were few Esquimouxs [sic] living in the region we explored."

Brackets are also used to enclose material that falls within material already enclosed by parentheses.

> The fall sales records are encouraging (see page 33, Monthly Sales [Table 2.1] for a detailed breakdown by product line).

Ellipses

Ellipses indicate that material has been omitted from a quotation or quoted material.

Original: This book describes the author's visit to Nepal and
                 renders scenes of the rugged, mountainous
                 countryside that will remain in the reader's mind
                 forever.

Condensed: This book . . . renders scenes . . . that will remain in
                 the reader's mind forever.

When words are omitted at the end of a sentence, use an end mark plus
the ellipses.

Condensed: This book . . . renders scenes of the rugged,
                 mountainous countryside. . . .

Italics

Italics are used to indicate emphasis, to mark foreign terms and expressions not commonly used, and to highlight titles of publications and names of certain vehicles such as ships, spacecraft, and the like.

Emphasis

Occasionally, italics are used to stress certain words or phrases. This usage is more common in dialogue than in formal writing and should be kept to a minimum.

"I didn't want *blue* paint; I wanted *lavender* paint!"
"Mr. Lloyd, you told the prosecutor that you didn't meet Mrs. Young
    until last month. Is that right?"
On the basis of the field inspector's report, I recommend that *we shut
    down offshore drilling platform #45.*

Foreign Words and Phrases

Foreign words and phrases that are not part of common usage are
italicized.

The motto of the Marine Corps is *Semper Fidelis*—always faithful.
As they say, *ende gut, alles gut*: all's well that ends well.

However, many foreign words have been in common use long enough that they are no longer italicized. Check the dictionary for the latest usage.

Her paintings were very **avant-garde**.
At one time the motto **caveat emptor**—let the buyer beware—was the
   rule in business.
Her clothes are **chic**, her decor **passé**.
The military **junta** declared a 7:00 PM curfew.

Titles

The titles of plays, books, magazines, newspapers, movies, and other types of periodicals and publications are italicized when they appear in print. If the first word of a title is *a, an,* or *the,* it is italicized only if it is part of the actual name.

The Wall Street Journal (newspaper)	*Esquire* (magazine)
the *Los Angeles Times* (newspaper)	*Spider-Man* (movie)
Angels in America (play)	*Redbook* (magazine)
The Insider (corporate publication)	*The Da Vinci Code* (book)
Editorial Eye (newsletter)	

Vehicles

Use italics for the names of ships, spacecraft, airplanes, and other well-known vehicles.

the battleship *Excalibur*
the spaceship *Enterprise*
the shuttle *Columbia*
the *Titanic*
the President's jet *Air Force One*

Titles of Paintings in Italics.

Sentences and Sentence Patterns

The English language provides considerable flexibility in sentence construction. Using various sentence patterns produces speech and writing that are lively and interesting. Also, variety in sentence construction contributes to well-organized messages. (See Chapter 6 for more on sentence patterns.)

This chapter explains the building blocks of sentences—phrases and clauses, subjects and predicates—and the various ways sentences are constructed.

Sentences, Fragments, and Run-Ons

A *sentence* is a group of words that expresses a complete thought. It begins with a capital letter and closes with an end mark, either a period, a question mark, or an exclamation point. Sentences are classified as declarative (a statement), interrogative (a question), imperative (command or request), or exclamatory (for emphasis).

Declarative: We reached the final level of *Doom*.
Interrogative: How did you get past the Valley of Fire?
Imperative: Click on the dragon. Watch out for the Black Guard.
Exclamatory: I'm in the Secret Chamber!

Not every group of words is a sentence. A *fragment* is a phrase or clause that looks like a sentence but does not express a complete thought.

Fragment: down by the river where the fish bite
if he would just think

By themselves, fragments make little sense and leave important questions unanswered. Who or what is *down by the river where the fish bite*? What would happen *if he would just think*? Fragments must be joined with other sentence parts to form a complete thought.

Sentence: **We were** down by the river where the fish bite.
He could save himself so much trouble if he would just think.

Unlike fragments, which haven't enough parts to make a complete sentence, *run-ons* have too many parts. They are two or more complete thoughts—at times only vaguely related—strung together without punctuation.

Run-On: We have only three days until the trip starts I don't have my jacket repaired yet and that will take at least a day or so to do don't you think?

Run-on sentences can be corrected in a number of ways: by inserting the proper punctuation, by breaking the sentence into two or more smaller sentences, or by rewriting the sentence to eliminate the run-on.

Revised: We have only three days until the trip starts, and I forgot to have my jacket repaired. Do you think the repairs will take more than a day or so?
We have only three days to get ready for the trip. I forgot to have my jacket repaired. Do you think the repairs will take more than a day or so?

Phrases and Clauses

The various parts of speech are grouped into phrases and clauses, which make up the basic sentence.

Phrases

Phrases are groups of related words that do not contain a subject-verb combination or express a complete thought. There are noun, prepositional, participial, verb, and infinitive phrases.

Noun:	my widescreen TV	the tired old man
Prepositional:	over the wall	around the block
Participial:	playing the fool	running the program
Verb:	will be given	is coming
Infinitive:	to think	to draw

Clauses

Clauses are groups of related words that contain a subject-verb combination. *Independent clauses* express a complete thought and can stand by themselves as sentences. *Subordinate clauses* serve as part of a sentence but do not express a complete thought and cannot stand by themselves. They are subordinate to independent clauses.

Independent clauses:	the floodplain was completely underwater
	John got us jobs as stagehands
	they took the off-road trail
Subordinate clauses:	by the time June arrived
	because he works at the theater
	when they came to the turn
Complete sentences:	**By the time June arrived**, the floodplain was completely underwater.
	John got us jobs as stagehands, **because he works at the theater.**
	When they came to the turn, they took the off-road trail.

Subject and Predicate

The *subject* is the person, place, or thing that is the topic of the sentence. The *predicate* is what is said about the subject.

Subject	Predicate
The balloon	floated up through the trees.
New York City	is a major cultural center.
The zoo worker	was attacked by a tiger.

In most cases, as in the preceding examples, the subject of a sentence comes first, followed by the predicate. However, there are instances when the subject is placed after the predicate, omitted from the sentence, or placed inside the verb.

Into the valley of death rode **the six hundred**. (subject follows the predicate)

Wash the car by tonight. (subject *you* is understood)

Are **your parents** coming tomorrow? (subject is placed inside the verb)

There are **three ships** coming into the bay. (*There* occupies the place of the subject, but *three ships* is still the subject of the sentence.)

Forms of the Subject

The most common forms of the subject are nouns, pronouns, and proper nouns.

The **stock market** is strong right now.

Why don't **you** pick up some lettuce for tonight?

Carol almost flunked algebra this semester.

At times, noun phrases and clauses, gerunds and gerund phrases, and infinitive phrases can also function as the subject.

Noun phrase:	**The girl on the swing** is my niece.
Noun clause:	**What they said** isn't true.

Gerund:	**Swimming** is a major Olympic sport.
Gerund phrase:	**Playing chess** kept him occupied for hours.
Infinitive phrase:	**To see clearly** is an artist's greatest task.

Complete Subject. The noun or pronoun and all its modifiers are known as the *complete subject*.

The ship in the harbor seemed small and frail.
What he said in the car surprised us all.
The trees, which had been damaged in the storm, were cut down
   the next day.

Simple and Compound Subjects. The noun or pronoun is known as the *simple subject*. It is important to identify the subject because it controls the form of the verb used in the sentence.

The **ship** in the harbor seemed small and frail.
Daffodils open in early spring.
The **trees**, which had been damaged in the storm, were cut down the
   next day.

The *compound subject* is composed of two or more nouns, pronouns, or phrases or clauses to express the topic of a sentence.

Nouns:	The **Democrats** and **Republicans** fought a bitter campaign.
Pronouns:	**She** and **I** used to be best friends.
Noun clauses:	**What he wanted** and **what he got** were two different things.
Gerund phrases:	**Working at home** and **commuting electronically** are more popular now.

Forms of the Predicate

The predicate always contains a verb. An action verb generally will have an object as well as various verb modifiers. A linking verb will have a complement along with its verb modifiers. Thus, the predicate usually is composed of a verb, object or complement, and verb modifiers.

Predicate with Action Verbs. The most common form of predicate is one in which the verb describes some sort of action. The verb is followed by a direct object (DO) and, in some cases, by an indirect object (IO).

IO   DO
Indiana Jones sent his **partner** the secret **code**.

DO   DO
I brought four **sandwiches** and one **pizza**.

DO
Michael Phelps won six gold **medals** in the 2004 summer Olympics.

IO   DO
She gave **him** a **rose**.

Note: the object of a preposition is never an indirect object.

DO   O OF PREP
She gave a **rose** to **him**.

Some action verbs can drop their objects and still make sense. The predicate then consists of the verb only.

They **have been practicing**.
We **were reading**.
The reporter **disappeared**.
The weather **changed**.

Action verbs can also take complements. Nouns, pronouns, prepositional phrases, adjectives, and verb phrases can serve as complements in the predicate.

He taught the dog **to roll over**. (The infinitive phrase *to roll over* is the complement.)

I called him a **prince**. (The noun *prince* is the complement.)

They made camp **on the hill**. (The prepositional phrase *on the hill* is the complement.)

She acted her part **beautifully**. (The adverb *beautifully* is the complement.)

We saw the tornado **heading this way**. (The participial phrase *heading this way* is the complement.)

She lay **down in the tall grass**. (The adverb *down* and the prepositional phrase *in the tall grass* are the complement and indicate direction and location.)

Predicate with Linking Verbs. Linking verbs that express being, seeming, or becoming need a predicate adjective or verb complement to complete them. The more common of these verbs include *seem, become, grow, taste, smell, appear, look, feel,* and *sound.*

He seems **nervous**. (*He seems* is incomplete. The adjective *nervous* acts as the predicate adjective.)

I feel **that you should apologize for your outburst**. (The noun clause *that you should apologize for your outburst* is the verb complement.)

Compound Predicate. At times a sentence will contain more than one verb, object, or complement. These structures are known as *compound verbs, compound objects,* and *compound complements.*

The rookie **hits** and **fields** like Ichiro Suzuki. (Two verbs function as the compound verb.)

I gave away my **coat** and **boots**. (The two nouns *coat* and *boots* serve as the compound direct object of the verb *gave*.)

Mark's first week abroad was **long** and **lonely**. (The two adjectives *long* and *lonely* are the compound complement.)

Sentence Constructions

English has four basic sentence constructions: simple, compound, complex, and compound-complex. Each construction uses the same basic elements of sentence structure—parts of speech, phrases, and clauses.

Simple Sentence

The *simple sentence* is an independent clause with no subordinate clauses. It begins with a capital letter and closes with an end mark. Simple sentences can vary considerably in length.

> I bought four apples at the farmers' market.
> I bought four apples, a basket of tomatoes, a bag of green beans, and three squashes at the farmers' market.
> The farmers' market is a classic example of producers selling directly to consumers and avoiding the attempts of agents to control the supply or to manipulate the price.

Compound Sentence

The *compound sentence* contains two or more independent clauses but no subordinate clauses. The two independent clauses usually are joined by a comma followed by a conjunction (*and, but, nor, yet*). They may also be joined by a semicolon, a semicolon followed by a linking adverb (*therefore, however, because, since*), or a colon.

Conjunction:	I don't know where he went, <u>and</u> no one has seen him since this afternoon.
Semicolon:	Harold the First fought in northern Ireland; his campaigns generally were successful.
Linking adverb:	Vivian wanted to stay another week in Ashville; <u>however,</u> her parents refused to send her more money.
Colon:	You must have heard the news: we're all getting bonuses this year!

Complex Sentence

The *complex sentence* is made up of an independent clause and one or more subordinate clauses. When a subordinate clause introduces the sentence, it is usually followed by a comma unless it is very short. In the following examples, the subordinate clauses are printed in bold type.

> The library closes early in summer **when the students are out of school.**
> **After the clear days of Indian summer,** the autumn skies grow heavy and dark.
> Linda told us on the phone **that they had had a flat tire last night and that the car wouldn't start this morning.**
> **When you come in the front door,** make sure you push it shut, **because the lock doesn't always catch.**

Compound-Complex Sentence

The *compound-complex sentence* is composed of two or more independent clauses and one or more subordinate clauses. In the examples, the subordinate clauses are printed in bold type.

> John Lennon wrote many ballads, and he recorded them **while he was in England.**
> The letter carrier, **who is always punctual,** didn't come today; I wonder if she is ill.
> He should call you **as soon as he arrives;** but **if you don't hear from him,** let me know.

Modifiers in Sentences

A *modifier* is any word or group of words that limits or qualifies the meaning of other parts of the sentence. Be sure that your modifiers are clearly joined to the word or words they qualify. Descriptive phrases or clauses joined to the wrong words are known as *dangling modifiers.*

You can correct dangling modifiers by making the doer of the action the subject of the sentence, by adding omitted words, or by changing the phrase to a subordinate clause.

Incorrect: Coming over the hill, the blueberries were seen in the valley below.

Correct: As we came over the hill, **we saw** the blueberries in the valley below.

Incorrect: Referring to your request of April 12, the matter is being reviewed by our board.

Correct: **Our board is reviewing** your request of April 12.

Incorrect: When she was four years old, her mother died. (Was her mother four years old?)

Correct: **She was four years old when** her mother died.

Incorrect: Exhausted and bleary-eyed, the report was finished by the team in the morning. (Was the report exhausted and bleary-eyed?)

Correct: **The team**, exhausted and bleary-eyed, **finished the report in the morning.**

Capitalization, Abbreviations, and Numbers

Rules for capitalization, abbreviations, and numbers can be confusing. Not all grammar books agree on the same style. The guidelines in this book are based on the latest accepted usage for business and personal writing.

Capitalization

Capitalize the first word in any sentence, the personal pronoun *I*, and the first word of a direct quotation if it is a complete statement.

Night falls quickly in the mountains.
The door was open when I arrived home.
He looked at the cake and said, "Diets, like pie crust, are made to be broken."

Proper Nouns and Adjectives

Capitalize all proper nouns and adjectives such as the names of persons, business firms, business products, institutions, government bodies and agencies, and public and private organizations.

Personal names:	Lance Armstrong, Barbara Walters
Business firm:	Wal-Mart, Mrs. Field's Cookies
Business products:	Honda Civic, Downy, Dr Pepper

Institutions:	Adler Planetarium, Stanford University
Government bodies and agencies:	Internal Revenue Service, Civil Rights Commission, Office of Homeland Security
Public organizations:	Junior Chamber of Commerce, Girl Scouts of America
Private organizations:	Midwest Authors Guild, JoAnn Kilmer Foundation
Proper adjectives:	**Canadian** beer, **American** flag, **Australian** kangaroo

Hyphenated Names and Prefixes

Capitalize all hyphenated names and hyphenated proper nouns. Also capitalize all proper nouns and adjectives used with a prefix, but do not capitalize the prefix.

Send the bill to Mrs. **Simon-Allen**.

The **Minneapolis-St. Paul** project has been approved.

I am neither **anti-British** nor **pro-French**; I happen to enjoy both countries equally well.

He will always be a pro-**Chicago** politician.

Family Relationships

Capitalize words describing family relationships only when they substitute for a proper noun or are used with the person's name. Do not capitalize the words if they are used with a possessive pronoun.

I told **Aunt Julia** that **my sister** would be late.

She described **her father** to me perfectly.

Granny Winters and **Grampa McDonough** live in the same neighborhood.

We got a letter from **Aunt Helen** and **Uncle Bill**.

Do you know **her cousin Lucia**?

Nationalities and Races

Capitalize the names of nationalities. Racial groups may be lowercased or capitalized. The only firm rule is *be consistent*. If you capitalize one racial group, capitalize the others as well.

Nationalities	Racial Groups
Australian	Black *or* black
Chinese	White *or* white
Indian	
Thai	

Languages and School Subjects

Capitalize languages and those school subjects followed by a number. Do not capitalize general school subjects unless the subject is a language.

Languages	School Subjects
Arabic	Biology 403
English	French
Korean	history
Polish	literature
	Social Science 202
	conversational Spanish
	statistics

Religious Names and Terms

The names of all religions, denominations, and local groups are capitalized.

Religions

Buddhism	Islam	Shintoism
Christianity	Judaism	Taoism
Hinduism		

Denominations and Movements

Jehovah's Witnesses	Mormonism	Theosophy
Methodism	Sufism	Zen Buddhism

Local Groups

Church of the Redeemer	Saint Leonard's House
Midwest Baptist Conference	Temple Shalom

Capitalize the names of deities and revered persons.

the Almighty	Child of God	the Word
Allah	Jehovah	Logos
Lamb of God	Holy Ghost	Mother of God
Pan	Shiva	Kwan Yin
Kali	Egun-gun	Astarte

Capitalize the names of sacred works or highly revered works and their individual parts.

the Bible	the Koran	the Book of David
the Talmud	the Vedas	the Tripitaka
Genesis	the Beatitudes	the Diamond Sutra
Apostles' Creed	Epistles	Sermon on the Mount
the Decalogue	Book of Job	Acts of the Apostles

Capitalize religious holidays and terms relating to the Eucharistic sacrament.

Ascension of the Virgin	High Mass	Passover
Christmas	Holy Communion	Ramadan
Easter	Lent	Yom Kippur

Names of other rites and services are not capitalized in a text.

baptism	confirmation	seder
bar (bas) mitzvah	evening prayer	vesper service
confession	matins	worship service

Academic Degrees and Personal Titles

Capitalize academic degrees and personal titles used as part of people's names or as a substitute for their names. Titles used after a person's name or by themselves generally are not capitalized.

The exception to the rule occurs when the title refers to the highest national, state, or church offices, such as the President of the United States. In such cases, the title may be capitalized.

Professor Louise Sasaki	Louise Sasaki, PhD
Dr. Bernard Stone	Bernard Stone, MD
President Don Roth	Don Roth, president
Director Ellen Tate	Ellen Tate, director
Vice President Johnson	the Vice President (of the United States)
Cardinal Cody	the Cardinal
Pope Benedict XVI	the Pope
Reverend Alice Milano	the reverend
General George Custer	the general
Admiral Patricia Tracey	the admiral
Queen Elizabeth	the Queen
Count von Moltke	the count

Historic Events, Special Events, and Holidays

Capitalize the names of historic events and periods, special events, holidays, and other publicly recognized special days.

Battle of Midway	Miami Book Fair
Black History Month	Mother's Day
Columbus Day	National Pickle Week
Elizabethan Age	New Year's Day
Han Dynasty	Nicene Council
Hundred Years' War	Presidents' Day
Labor Day	Thanksgiving
Live AID Africa	World War II

Historical Monuments, Places, and Buildings

Capitalize the names of all historical monuments, places, and buildings.

Arlington National Cemetery	the Prudential Building
the Chicago Loop	Times Square
the Latin Quarter	Washington Monument

Calendar Days, Months, and Seasons

Capitalize the names of all days of the week and months of the year. Seasons of the year are lowercase unless they are personified.

Tuesday	Wednesday	Friday
November	June	April
fall	winter	summer

But: Have we not seen, Summer, your jeweled nights, your days young and fair?

Documents

Capitalize the first word and all other words except articles (*a, an, the*) and prepositions under five letters (*in, to, out*) in charters, treaties, declarations, laws, and other official documents. However, when the words *charter, act, treaty,* and *law* are used alone, they generally are not capitalized.

Articles of Incorporation	Treaty of Orleans
Declaration of Independence	Uniform Commercial Code
Magna Carta	Wanger Act

Titles of Publications

Capitalize the first word and all other words except articles and prepositions under five letters in the titles of books, chapters, magazines, articles, newspapers, musical compositions, and other publications.

The Handmaid's Tale (opera)
Harry Potter and the Chamber of Secrets (book)
"The Midwest's Blue-Collar Blues" (article)
"Do Your Own Tune-Ups" (chapter)
Kansas City Star (newspaper)

Compass Points

Points of the compass are not capitalized when they refer simply to direction or are used as adjectives. They are capitalized when they refer to regions of the country.

east	north	southwest	eastern
west	south	northwest	western
the South	the East	the Southwest	the Northeast
the North Central states			

Geographic Names and Regions

Capitalize all geographic names and regions of a country, continent, or hemisphere.

Cities, Townships, Countries, States, Continents

California	New York	South America
India	Niles Township	Western Hemisphere

Islands, Peninsulas, Straits, Beaches

Baja Peninsula	Strait of Magellan	Myrtle Beach
Canary Islands	Strait of Malacca	Padre Island

Bodies of Water

Aegean Sea	Nile River	Victoria Falls
Lake Tahoe	Tinker Creek	Walden Pond

Mountains and Mountain Chains

the Andes	Kilimanjaro	Mount Fuji
Cascade Mountains	Mount Everest	Pikes Peak

Parks, Forests, Canyons, Dams

Aswan Dam	Humboldt Redwoods Forest
Bright Angel Canyon	Serengeti National Preserve
Three Gorges Dam	Yosemite National Park

Scientific Terms

The rules for capitalizing scientific terms, particularly the division of plants and animals, can be complex and bewildering. This section presents some general rules for capitalizing the more common terms that are likely to be used.

Common Names of Plants and Animals. Usually, lowercase the name of plants and animals, capitalizing only proper nouns and adjectives used with the names. Check a dictionary to be sure of accuracy.

black-eyed Susan	rhesus monkey
Cooper's hawk	Rhode Island red
border collie	Rocky Mountain sheep
golden retriever	rose of Sharon
jack-in-the-pulpit	Thomson's gazelle
mustang	thoroughbred
Persian cat	white leghorn fowl

Geological Terms. Capitalize the names of eras, periods, epochs, and episodes but not the words *era, period,* and so on used with the term.

Ice Age (reference to Pleistocene glacial epoch)	
Lower Jurassic period	Pliocene epoch
Paleozoic era	Cambrian period

Astronomical Terms. Capitalize all proper names of asteroids, planets and their satellites, constellations, and other astronomical phenomena. In many cases, *earth, sun,* and *moon* are lowercased unless used with other planets in a sentence.

Alpha Centauri	the Crab Nebula	Milky Way
Andromeda Galaxy	Demos	North Star
Arcturus	Halley's Comet	Orion
Big Dipper	the Leonids	Pleiades
Cassiopeia	Mercury	Saturn

Descriptive terms that apply to astronomical or meteorological phenomena are not capitalized.

aurora borealis	meteor shower
blizzard	sun dogs
hurricane	tornado
the rings of Jupiter	the moons of Uranus

Medical Terms. Lowercase the names of diseases, syndromes, symptoms, tests, drugs, and the like. Capitalize only proper nouns and adjectives or trade names used with these terms.

aspirin	Parkinson's disease
finger-nose test	poliomyelitis
Guillain-Barré syndrome	Salk vaccine
infectious granuloma	tetracycline
acetaminophen	Tylenol

Physical and Chemical Terms. Lowercase laws, theorems, principles, and the like, capitalizing only proper nouns and adjectives used with these terms. Chemical symbols are also capitalized and set without periods.

Boyle's law	Maxwell's equations
C^{14} or C-14	Newton's second law
carbon 14	Planck's constant
general theory of relativity	sulfuric acid
H_2SO_4	U^{238} or U-238
Lorenz transformations	uranium 238

Capitals with Numbers

Capitalize a noun or abbreviation before a number when it designates a formal part of a written work.

Act V, Scene 3	Paragraph 3 or Para. 3
Book IV	Section 44 or Sec. 44
Chapter 14 or Chap. 14	Unit 3

Abbreviations

The style for abbreviations has gone through a series of changes in the past few decades. The trend today is to drop the periods from most abbreviations used in writing. Within a document, however, periods may be used or omitted if the writer is consistent. For example, if *AM* appears without periods in one sentence, do not use *A.M.* in another.

General Guidelines

Here are some general guidelines for using abbreviations.

1. For formal and business writing, internal periods are omitted for most abbreviations related to time, academic degrees, metric measures, organizations, institutions, and government agencies.

2. Except for personal names and titles, abbreviations with internal periods (e.g., N.W.) should not have a space after the first period.

3. For abbreviations of personal names and titles, insert a space after the first period. (H. G. Wells, Lt. Col. Brice)

4. When in doubt about how to style abbreviations of personal or company names, always check with the individual or firm to see how they prefer the abbreviation to be written.

Personal Names and Titles

This section presents some general rules for the abbreviation of personal names and titles.

Personal Names. Avoid using abbreviations for given names except when transcribing a signature.

> Dorothy Brandt *not* Dor. Brandt
> Charles Villiard *not* Chas. Villiard

If the signature is written with abbreviations, follow the style of the author.

> Yours truly, Geo. C. Kelly
> Sincerely yours, L. K. Geng

Some publications and business writers omit the periods following initials. However, for convenience and clarity it is usually good practice to use periods with all initials given with names.

> Caroline S. Wilson　　Robert J. Edwards
> T. J. Warshell　　　　A. Teresa Valdez

If the person is referred to by initials only, no periods are used.

> FDR (Franklin Delano Roosevelt)
> LBJ (Lyndon Baines Johnson)
> HD (Hilda Doolittle)

Titles Before Names. Social titles are always abbreviated whether used with the surname only or the full name. Notice which titles are used with or without periods. If you are in doubt about when to use periods with a social title, consult an up-to-date dictionary.

Mrs. Gloria Greenberg	Mr. Valentine Cancilleri
Ms. Barbara Walnum	M. Tricia (Thomas) Benton
Mme Cecilia Payne	Mlle Jane Tild
Messrs. Paul Mori and Norman Zuefle	Dr. Evelyn Veach

When a civil or military title is used with the surname alone, it is spelled out. When the full name is used, the title is abbreviated.

Senator Obama	Sen. Barack Obama
Alderperson Abuelos	Ald. Yvonne Abuelos
Representative Rush	Rep. Carlton J. Rush

The military now uses all capitals and no periods to abbreviate titles. However, the conventional spelling of military titles is still used in most forms of civilian writing. Notice that there is a space after the first period in an abbreviated title.

Lieutenant Colonel Claire	LT COL Ruth Claire or Lt. Col. Ruth Claire
Staff Sergeant Oltman	SSG Frank Oltman or S. Sgt. Frank Oltman

The titles *Reverend* and *Honorable* are spelled out if they are preceded by *the*. They may also be used with social titles. *Reverend* is never used with the surname alone, but the title may be abbreviated when used with the person's full name.

the Reverend Betty J. Dell	Rev. Betty J. Dell
the Right Reverend Monsignor Carl L. Bernard	Rt. Rev. Msr. Carl L. Bernard
the Honorable Wilson O. Justman	Hon. Wilson O. Justman

Titles After Names. Titles, degrees, affiliations, or the designation *Jr.* (junior), *Sr.* (senior), or *II, III* (or *2d, 3d*) following a person's name are considered part of that name. While the abbreviations *Jr.* and *Sr.* are set off from the name by commas, the designations *II, III, 2d,* or *3d* are not set off by commas. These abbreviations are used only with the full name, never just the surname (*Mr. Gregory Young, Jr.,* not *Mr. Young, Jr.*).

Njoki Salumbe, PhD	Richard Butzen, LLD
Daniel Cronon III, MA	Whitney Rune, Sr.

The abbreviation *Esq.* (*esquire*) refers to someone who is a lawyer and is never used when another title is given, whether before or after the name.

Sue Allen, Esq.	*not*	Ms. Sue Allen, Esq.
Carl Hanson, Esq.	*not*	Carl Hanson, Esq, PhD

Social titles are also dropped if another title is used following the name.

Harriet Long, MFA	*not*	Miss Harriet Long, MFA

Names with *Saint*. When *Saint* precedes the person's name, it is often abbreviated *St.,* although many prefer to spell the word out.

St. Catherine de Sienna   *or*   **Saint** Catherine de Sienna

Saint is generally omitted before the names of apostles, evangelists, and church founders.

Matthew	John	Luke	Mark
Paul	John the Baptist	Augustine	Jerome

When *Saint* is used as part of a personal name, follow the style preferred by the individual.

Ruth St. Denis
Adele St. Claire Hutchins
Alfred George Saint-Augustine

Company Names

The following abbreviations are commonly used as part of firm names.

& (and)	Inc. (incorporated)
Assoc. (association, associates, associated)	Ltd. (limited)
Bro., Bros. (brothers)	Mfg. (manufacturing)
Co. (company)	RR, Ry (railroad)
Corp. (corporation)	

Abbreviations of company names may or may not use periods. Make sure you determine how the company itself prefers to spell its name. Some of the more common abbreviations include the following:

IBM	Gor-Tex, Inc.
Ford Motor Co.	ATT
Warner Bros.	AOL
MCI	Canada NewsWire Ltd.

Agencies and Organizations

The names of government agencies, network broadcasting companies, associations, fraternal and service organizations, unions, and other groups are usually abbreviated without periods. However, some publications such as *The New York Times* still print them with periods. Whichever style you use, be sure you are consistent.

Unions

AFL-CIO (American Federation of Labor—Congress of Industrial Organizations)

UMW (United Mine Workers)

UAW (United Auto Workers)

Government Agencies

HHS (Department of Health and Human Services)

DOT (Department of Transportation)

CIA (Central Intelligence Agency)

Social Organizations

BSA (Boy Scouts of America)
YWCA (Young Women's Christian Association)
DAR (Daughters of the American Revolution)
VFW (Veterans of Foreign Wars)

Professional Organizations

PEN (Poets, Editors, and Novelists)
AMA (American Medical Association)

Geographic Terms

In some cases geographic terms may be abbreviated in more than one way. As always, the key is to be consistent.

Address and State Abbreviations. Address abbreviations may be used with or without periods and may be set in all capitals or in initial capitals only. The U.S. Postal Service recommends using all capitals without periods for address abbreviations. Following is a list of the most common abbreviations used in addresses.

Avenue	AVE, Ave.	Point	PT, Pt.
Expressway	EXPY, Expy.	Ridge	RDG, Rdg.
Hospital	HOSP, Hosp.	River	RV, Rv.
Heights	HTS, Hts.	Road	RD, Rd.
Institute	INST, Inst.	Rural	R, R.
Junction	JCT, Jct.	Shore	SH, Sh.
Lake	LK, Lk.	Square	SQ, Sq.
Lakes	LKS, Lks.	Station	STA, Sta.
Lane	LN, Ln.	Terrace	TER, Ter.
Meadows	MDWS, Mdws.	Turnpike	TPKE, Tpke.
Mountains	MT, Mt.	Union	UN, Un.
Palms	PLMS, Plms.	View	VW, Vw.
Park	PK, Pk.	Village	VLG, Vlg.
Parkway	PKY, Pky.		

Points of the compass following a street name are used without periods. If they precede the name, periods are used.

147 Eastwood NW   1737 Fifth Street SE
6 N. Michigan   2320 E. Grand

Use the postal zip code abbreviations for states, territories, and the Canadian provinces. The abbreviations are capitalized and contain no punctuation.

STATE ABBREVIATIONS

Alabama	AL	Nebraska	NE
Alaska	AK	Nevada	NV
Arizona	AZ	New Hampshire	NH
Arkansas	AR	New Jersey	NJ
California	CA	New Mexico	NM
Colorado	CO	New York	NY
Connecticut	CT	North Carolina	NC
Delaware	DE	North Dakota	ND
Florida	FL	Ohio	OH
Georgia	GA	Oklahoma	OK
Hawaii	HI	Oregon	OR
Idaho	ID	Pennsylvania	PA
Illinois	IL	Rhode Island	RI
Indiana	IN	South Carolina	SC
Iowa	IA	South Dakota	SD
Kansas	KS	Tennessee	TN
Kentucky	KY	Texas	TX
Louisiana	LA	Utah	UT
Maine	ME	Vermont	VT
Maryland	MD	Virginia	VA
Massachusetts	MA	Washington	WA
Michigan	MI	West Virginia	WV
Minnesota	MN	Wisconsin	WI
Mississippi	MS	Wyoming	WY
Missouri	MO	District of Columbia	DC
Montana	MT		

FOREIGN ABBREVIATIONS

Puerto Rico	PR	Guam	GU
Alberta	AB	Virgin Islands	VI
Manitoba	MB	British Columbia	BC
Newfoundland	NF	New Brunswick	NB
Nova Scotia	NS	Northwest Territories	NT
Prince Edward Island	PE	Ontario	ON
Saskatchewan	SK	Quebec	PQ
Labrador	LB	Yukon Territory	YT

Names of Countries. The names of countries should be spelled out whenever possible. When abbreviated, however, periods should be used after each part of the name. There is generally no space after the first period.

England	Engl.
France	Fr.
Germany	Ger.
Italy	It.
Russia	Rus.
Spain	Sp.
Sweden	Swe.
United Kingdom	U.K. or G.B. (Great Britain)
United States	U.S.

For the correct abbreviations for other countries, consult a good dictionary or world atlas.

Place Names. Prefixes such as *Fort, Mount, Point,* and the like used with geographic names should not be abbreviated unless space must be saved in the text.

Fort Wayne	Ft. Wayne
Mount Everest	Mt. Everest
Point Townsend	Pt. Townsend
South Orange	S. Orange

Many grammarians make an exception for names beginning with *Saint* and abbreviate the prefix in all cases. However, the prefixes *San* and *Santa* are not abbreviated.

San Cristobal   St. Lawrence Seaway
Santa Barbara   St. Louis

Points of the Compass. The following symbols are used to abbreviate points of the compass.

N, S, E, W   NE, SE, NW, SW
S by SE   N by NW

Latitude and *longitude* are never abbreviated when used alone or in non-technical text. In technical notation, the terms are abbreviated without periods and the compass symbols inserted following the degrees of latitude and longitude.

the equatorial latitudes
longitude 22° west
lat 42°57′3″ N
long 90°27′5″ W

Time

Time designations may be abbreviated in more than one way. Remember to be consistent.

Time of Day. Abbreviations that indicate time of day or night may be set in all capitals or lowercase (or as small capitals).

AM, am, AM   (ante meridiem)   before noon
M, M   (meridian)   noon
PM, pm, PM   (post meridiem)   after noon

Days of the Week, Months of the Year. The names of the days of the week can be abbreviated in the following ways:

Monday	Mon. or M
Tuesday	Tues. or Tu
Wednesday	Wed. or W
Thursday	Thurs. or Th
Friday	Fri. or F
Saturday	Sat. or Sa
Sunday	Sun. or Su

Months of the year are abbreviated as follows:

January	Jan. or Jan or Ja
February	Feb. or Feb or F
March	Mar. or Mar or Mr
April	Apr. or Apr or Ap
May	May or My
June	June or Jun or Je
July	July or Jul or Jl
August	Aug. or Aug or Ag
September	Sept. or Sept or S
October	Oct. or Oct or O
November	Nov. or Nov or N
December	Dec. or Dec or D

Years. Accepted abbreviations mark the years before and after the birth of Christ.

The abbreviation AD (*anno Domini*—means in the year of the Lord) precedes the year.

William the Conqueror landed on British shores in **AD 1066.**

BC (before Christ) follows the year.

Alexander the Great died in the summer of **323 BC.**

Scholarly Abbreviations

The rules for use of abbreviations in scholarship are widely agreed upon and include the following:

1. Abbreviations should be kept out of the body of the text as much as possible, except in technical matters.

2. Abbreviations such as *e.g., i.e.,* and *etc.* should be used primarily in parenthetical material.

3. Scholarly abbreviations such as *ibid., cf., s.v.,* and *op. cit.* should be used only in footnotes, bibliographical material, and general notes to the text.

Following is a partial list of some of the more familiar scholarly abbreviations. For a complete list, consult a dictionary, scholarly handbook, or more detailed grammar text.

anon.	anonymous
biog.	biography
cf.	*confer*, compare
cont.	continued
def.	definition, definite
div.	division
e.g.	*exempli gratia*, for example
esp.	especially
hdqrs.	headquarters
i.e.	*id est*, that is
lit.	literally
mgr.	manager
ms.	manuscript
n.a.	not applicable, not available
pp.	pages
rev.	review, revised, revision
subj.	subject
trans.	translation, translated
vol.	volume
yr.	your, year

Measures

Abbreviations for units of measure are the same whether the unit is singular or plural.

English Measure. The abbreviations for length, area, and volume are followed by periods in nonscientific writing. The abbreviations are as follows:

Length		Area		Volume	
in.	inch	sq. in.	square inch	cu. in.	cubic inch
ft.	foot, feet	sq. ft.	square foot	cu. ft.	cubic foot
yd.	yard	sq. yd.	square yard	cu. yd.	cubic yard
rd.	rod	sq. rd.	square rod		
mi.	mile	sq. mi.	square mile		
		a.	acre		

Abbreviations for weight and capacity reflect the complicated English system of measures. There are three systems in use: *avoirdupois*, the common system; *troy*, used by jewelers; and *apothecaries'* measure. Although the metric system is being adopted in the United States, these other systems are still in use. The abbreviations are as follows:

Weight		Dry Measure		Liquid Measure	
gr.	grain	pt.	pint	min.	minim
s.	scruple	qt.	quart	fl. dr.	fluid dram
dr.	dram	pk.	peck	fl. oz.	fluid ounce
dwt.	pennyweight	bu.	bushel	gi.	gill
oz.	ounce	c.	cup	pt.	pint
lb.	pound	tsp.	teaspoon	qt.	quart
cwt.	hundredweight	tbl.	tablespoon	gal.	gallon
tn.	ton	bbl.	barrel		

English abbreviations for the standard units of time are as follows:

sec.	second	h., hr.	hour
min.	minute	d.	day
mo.	month	yr.	year

Metric System. The metric system, long used in scientific publications, is gradually becoming the national system of weights and measures. The basic units of measure are the liter, gram, and meter. The following abbreviations are used with metric measurements:

Length		Area		Volume	
mm	millimeter	sq. mm	square millimeter	mm³	cubic millimeter
cm	centimeter	sq. cm	square centimeter	cc	cubic centimeter
dm	decimeter	sq. dm	square decimeter	dm³	cubic decimeter
m	meter	sq. m	square meter	m³	cubic meter
dam	dekameter	sq. dam	square dekameter		
ca	centare	sq. ca	square centare		
ha	hectare	sq. ha	square hectare		
km	kilometer	sq. km	square kilometer		

Capacity		Weight	
ml	milliliter	mg	milligram
cl	centiliter	cg	centigram
dl	deciliter	dg	decagram
l	liter	g	gram
dal	dekaliter	dag	dekagram
hl	hectoliter	hg	hectogram
kl	kiloliter	kg	kilogram

Science and Technology

The International System of Units (SI) is generally used by scientists around the world to label measurements. SI is roughly equivalent to the metric system. In some cases, however, the method of forming abbreviations differs among the various disciplines of science. For a full listing of scientific abbreviations, consult a technical handbook or scientific style book.

Following are the seven fundamental SI units, termed base units, that serve as the foundation terms in science.

Term	Unit	Abbreviation
length	meter	m
mass	kilogram	kg
time	second	s
electric current	ampere	A
thermodynamic temperature	kelvin	K
amount of substance	mole	mol
luminous intensity	candela	cd

The abbreviations used by various branches of science may or may not be related to the International System. Following is a partial list of the more commonly used abbreviations. Notice that they are set without periods.

AC	alternating current	AM	amplitude modulation
AU	astronomic unit	BP	boiling point
cal	calorie	CP	candle power
CPS	cycles per second	DC	direct current
FM	frequency modulation	HP	horsepower
kw	kilowatt	MPG	miles per gallon
pH	acidity of alkalinity	RPM	revolutions per minute
std	standard	temp	temperature
UT, UTC	universal time		

Commercial Abbreviations

Abbreviations used in business and commerce follow a varied style. The most commonly used abbreviations and their accepted styles are given here.

acct.	account	agt.	agent
a/v	ad valorem	bal.	balance
bbl.	barrel	bdl.	bundle
bu.	bushel	c.l.	carload
COD	cash on delivery	cr.	credit, creditor
cwt.	hundredweight	doz.	dozen
dr.	debit, debitor	ea.	each
f.o.b., FOB	free on board	gro.	gross

Numbers

As in the case with capitalization and abbreviations, the rules for handling numbers in text are complex and varied. In this book, we provide guidelines that are generally agreed upon by many experts.

Arabic Numbers and Roman Numerals

Most of the figures used today are expressed in Arabic numbers. However, Roman numerals are still used in names, documents, books, dates, and so on. Following is a list of Arabic numbers and their equivalents in Roman numerals.

Arabic	Roman	Arabic	Roman	Arabic	Roman
1	I	16	XVI	90	XC
2	II	17	XVII	100	C
3	III	18	XVIII	200	CC
4	IV	19	XIX	300	CCC
5	V	20	XX	400	CD
6	VI	21	XXI	500	D
7	VII	22	XXII	600	DC
8	VIII	23	XXIII	700	DCC
9	IX	24	XXIV	800	DCCC
10	X	25	XXV	900	CM
11	XI	26	XXVI	1,000	M
12	XII	27	XXVII	2,000	MM
13	XIII	28	XXVIII	3,000	MMM
14	XIV	29	XXIX	4,000	$M\overline{V}$
15	XV	30	XXX	5,000	$\overline{V}$

Figures or Words

Whether numbers should be spelled out or written in figures depends on several factors. Among them are the size of the number, what it stands for, and what kind of text it appears in—business, personal, scientific, or scholarly.

In general, use the "rule of ten" in determining whether to spell out a number or express it in figures. Under the rule of ten, spell out numbers ten and under (two, five, seven) and any number that is divisible by ten (twenty, sixty, eighty). All other numbers over ten are written in figures.

> Governors from **six** states urged passage of the water-rights bill.
> I ordered **three** dozen boxes of mint candies.
> Did you know this book has **1,345** pages?
> She turned **39** last year but doesn't look over **25**.
> Our flight will arrive in Hong Kong in **12** hours.
> We now have a **thirty**-year mortgage to pay off.

Round Numbers. Numbers used as approximations in place of specific figures are often spelled out, even when expressed as hundreds of thousands.

> The march drew an estimated **thirty-one thousand** people.
> About **three** to **four hundred thousand** people were left homeless by the floods.
> Some form of sun worship has existed in human culture for nearly **twelve thousand years**.

Very large numbers are usually expressed in figures followed by *million, billion, trillion,* and so on.

> It would cost **$3.5 billion** to send a piloted probe to Jupiter.
> The gross national product is nearly **$257 trillion**.
> The greater metropolitan Chicago area contains more than **7.2 million** people.

Ordinal Numbers. The same rule of ten holds for ordinal numbers (*first, second, third*) as well.

Luciano ranked **fifth** in a class of 356 students.
My two horses came in **first** and **ninth** in the afternoon race.
The **25th** article in the bylaws hasn't been revised.
Bjorn was given the **232d** and **233d** numbers out of 655.

Notice that the form for *second* and *third* is *d* and not *nd* or *rd*.

Consistency. The exception to the rule of ten occurs when numbers under and over ten are used in a series or to refer to the same item in a sentence or paragraph. For the sake of consistency, numbers under ten are frequently expressed in figures.

Joan's family has **5** children, **11** cats, **3** turtles, **15** gerbils, and **2** canaries.
In **ten** years, the population has grown from about **8,000** to **154,567**. (*Ten* is spelled out because it is not related to the population figures but stands by itself. Compare that sentence to *In the past 10 to 15 years, the population has grown from about 8,000 to 154,567.* In this case, the figure *10* is used because it is related to the same category—years—as the number *15*.)
We climbed the **102**-story building all the way to the top, but **four** of us had trouble making the last **2 or 3** stories. (The figures *2* and *3* refer to the same item—the number of stories. *Four,* however, refers to a separate category, the number of people, and is therefore spelled out.)

Numbers Together. In some instances, numbers are used next to each other for more than one item in a sentence. Generally, to avoid confusion, the smaller of the two figures will be expressed in words.

We developed **twenty-five 35 mm** slides yesterday.
The stock cars will go **14 two-mile** laps.

I'd like **250 thirty-seven-cent** stamps.
He bought **twelve 65-cent** labels.

First Word in Sentence. Spell out numbers that begin a sentence, regardless of any inconsistency this may create in the rest of the sentence or paragraph. As a general rule, if the sentence contains more than one figure, or if the figure is large, try to rephrase the sentence so that the number does not come first.

Twenty-seven people attended the banquet.
Fifteen cars piled up on the freeway, and **37** cars blocked the exit
   ramp.

Avoid:	**Twenty** out of every **100** people interviewed preferred daytime baseball games.
Better:	Daytime baseball games were preferred by **20** out of every **100** people interviewed.
	or
	We found that **20** out of every **100** people interviewed preferred daytime baseball games.
Avoid:	**Nineteen twenty-seven** marked the first solo transatlantic flight in aviation history.
Better:	The year **1927** marked the first solo transatlantic flight in aviation history.

Ages

Express exact ages in figures. Approximate ages can be expressed in words or figures, but be sure to use the same style throughout.

Theodore Roosevelt was elected Vice President when he was only **42**.
Andrea is **7** and Van is **14**.
The baby is **2** years and **6** months old.
She was about **sixty** when she first traveled to Africa.
My father is nearly **ninety**.

Names

Roman numerals are used to distinguish among members of the same family who have identical names. No comma is used between the name and Roman numerals.

John Ellis **III**   Bror von Blixen **IV**

Roman numerals are also used to differentiate sovereigns, emperors, and popes with the same name. Modern usage, however, permits Arabic numerals in some cases.

John **XXIII** or John **23d**
Elizabeth **II**
Richard **III**

Vehicles such as ships, spacecraft, cars, and airplanes may also be given Roman numerals to distinguish them from previous models with the same name. Although earlier spacecraft in the NASA program carried Roman numerals, current practice is to use Arabic numbers.

*America **IV***   *Bluebird **III***
*Mercury **II***   *Apollo **12***
*Bell X-**15***   *Saturn **2***

Governmental Designations

Unlike with the "rule of ten," whether numbers are spelled out in governmental designations often depends on whether they are less than one hundred.

Governments. Ordinal numbers are used to designate particular dynasties, governments, and governing bodies in a succession. The numbers are spelled out if they are less than one hundred and precede the noun. In most cases, they are capitalized.

The **102d** Congress	**Third** Reich
First Continental Congress	**Twelfth** Dynasty
Eighty-sixth Congress	**Fourth** Republic

Political Divisions. Numbers one hundred or less indicating political divisions should be spelled out in ordinal form and capitalized.

Forty-second Ward	**Thirty-fifth** Precinct
123d Congressional District	Circuit Court of Appeals for the **Sixth** Court

Military Units. Spell out in ordinal form numbers one hundred or less that indicate military subdivision.

The **101st** Airborne	**Eighty-sixth** Regiment
156th Fighter Wing	**Seventh** Fleet
Second Battalion	**110th** Artillery

Organizations

Here are guidelines for using numbers in the names of organizations.

Unions and Lodges. Use Arabic numbers to express figures designating local branches of labor unions and of fraternal lodges.

Masonic Lodge No. **335**
Flight Attendants Union Local No. **127**
American Legion Post No. **34**

Churches. Spell out ordinal numbers used with religious organizations or houses of worship.

First United Methodist Church
Seventh-day Adventists
Twenty-second Church of Christ, Scientist
Second Baptist Church

Corporations and Civic Events. Numbers used in the names of companies or civic events may be spelled out or expressed in Arabic or Roman numerals. You will need to follow the particular organization's style.

Fifth Third Bank   **1st** Federal Savings & Loan
3rd Annual Sport Jamboree   **XXIV** Olympics

Addresses and Thoroughfares

House numbers should be expressed in figures, except for the number *one*. Numbered streets *one* through *ten* are spelled out.

One East Superior   **354** Crain Street
1274 **23d** Street   32 **Second** Avenue

When the address is part of a building's name, the number is usually spelled out.

One Magnificent Mile
Thirty-three Prudential Plaza

Use figures for all state and federal highways.

U.S. Route **66** (U.S. 66)
Interstate **294** (I-294)
Arizona **103**
County Line **24**

Time of Day

When time is expressed in even, half, or quarter hours, the numbers are generally spelled out.

The movie starts at a **quarter past four**.
I didn't get home until **twelve o'clock** last night.
The meeting is set for **two o'clock** this Thursday.

Figures are used when the exact time is given or in designations of time with AM or PM. Never use *o'clock* in either of these cases.

The train pulled into Lisbon at **12:33** in the morning.
The full report should be on the **6:30** news.
Precisely at **5:00**, I saw him leave his apartment.
We'll meet here again at **5:15 PM** tomorrow.
He called at **12:20 AM** to say he had locked himself out of his house.

In the 24-hour time system, figures are always used. There is no punctuation between the hour and minutes.

Our ship docks at **0615** on Wednesday.
Registration hours are from **0900** to **1130** and **1300** to **1530** every day except Sunday.

Dates

This section presents guidelines for the use of numbers in dates.

Day and Month. When writing dates, you can use either day/month/year or month/day/year.

On **7 August 1975**, we left for Egypt.
I sent the letter on **April 14, 1983**, but I never received a reply.

Notice that when the month/day/year form is used, the year is set off by commas before and after it.

When the day and month are used alone, references to another date in the same month are spelled out.

The order was dated **6 July**. We sent your package out on the **seventh**.

You may use either words or figures for the day when it occurs alone or when the month is part of a prepositional phrase in a sentence; just be consistent.

Paychecks are issued on the **5th** of each month.
Paychecks are issued on the **fifth** of each month.
On the **12th of April**, I signed the contract.
On the **twelfth of April**, I signed the contract.

Month and Year. When dates are identified only by month and year, no internal punctuation is necessary.

She entered school in **September 1979** when she turned 21.

The Year Alone or Abbreviated. Unless they begin a sentence, years are expressed in numbers no matter how large or small they may be. No commas are used in the figures.

The Egyptian Nile Valley was heavily populated by **3500 BC**.
Early records indicate the settlement was occupied from **34 BC** to
   AD 67.

Abbreviations of years drop the first two figures and substitute an apostrophe.

the class of **'69**
the spirit of **'76**
They were married in **'41**.

Centuries and Decades. References to particular centuries and decades are spelled out in lowercase letters (as long as there is no confusion about what century is being referenced).

We are at the beginning of the **twenty-first** century.
Social upheaval during the **sixties** gave way to political conservatism
   in the **eighties**.

If decades are identified by century, be sure to use the same style throughout.

Incorrect: The **1880s** and **'90s** were a time of colonial expansion.
Correct: The **1880s** and **1890s** were a time of colonial expansion.

Notice that there is no apostrophe before the final *s* after the year.

Eras. Use figures to express dates and words to express centuries whether the era designation comes before or after the date involved. The most frequently used era designations are as follows (notice no periods are used):

BC	before Christ (twelfth century BC)
AD	(*anno Domini*) in the year of the Lord (AD 1940)
AH	(*anno Hegirae*) in the year of (Muhammad's) Hegira (AH 736)
AH	(*anno Hebraico*) in the Hebrew year (AH 1426)
BCE	before the common era (2713 BCE)
BP	before the present (5892 BP)

The designations *AD* and *AH* precede the figures, while the other designations follow them. However, both AD and AH follow centuries expressed in words.

378 BC	AD 1945
13400 BP	AH 677
fourth century BC	fifteenth century AD

Money

Use figures to express sums of money whether foreign or U.S. currency. However, spell out small sums of money when the figure stands alone or serves as an adjective.

The car cost **$2,560.**
I changed **$4** for **£6.**
I remember when movies cost **twenty-five cents.**
They charge a **ten-dollar fee.**

If an abbreviation rather than a symbol is used for foreign currency, leave a space between the abbreviation and the figure.

When two currencies share the same symbol (for example, the *$* symbol in Canadian and U.S. money), use a prefix or suffix to distinguish between the two.

> His hotel bill totaled **$127.50 Canadian ($87.50 U.S.)** for a three-day stay.

Fractional and Large Amounts. Fractional amounts over one dollar are expressed in figures. Very large amounts may be expressed in figures and units of million, billion, or trillion.

> I bought this book for **$12.00** and then saw the same item on sale for **$3.50**.
> The clerk added up the charges of **$66.21, $43.90,** and **$23.10**.
> A painting valued at **$3.2 million** was stolen from the gallery.

Notice that when whole numbers and fractional amounts are used together, ciphers are used after the whole number (*$12.00, $3.50*).

Percentages

In general, percentages are expressed in figures followed by the word *percent*. In scientific and statistical material, the symbol % is used.

> Glenn's NOW account earns **7 percent** interest.
> There is a **50 percent** chance of snow tomorrow.
> Only **25%** of the blood samples tested yielded positive results.
> Power outages rose by **15%** during the summer months.

Fractions and Decimals

Mixed fractions and decimals are expressed in figures. For clarity, decimal fractions of less than 1.00 may be preceded by a zero.

24½ feet by **34¼** feet
up to **2.25** centimeters
a ration of **0.56** (or .56)
the CPI rose **1.5** percent

If several decimal fractions are used in a sentence or paragraph, make sure they have the same number of places to the right of the decimal point.

Incorrect: The variable rates for January were **.75** percent, **.4** percent, and **.96** percent.
Correct: The variable rates for January were **.75** percent, **.40** percent, and **.96** percent.

Simple fractions are expressed in words. If the fraction is used as an adjective, it is hyphenated. If it serves as a noun, it is two words.

one-fifth share of the market
two-thirds majority
one tenth of their income
one quarter of the workers

Measures

In scientific and many business texts, physical quantities such as distances, lengths, areas, volumes, pressures, weights, and the like are expressed in figures whether they are whole numbers or fractions.

125 miles	**87** meters
450 volts	**4** pounds **10** ounces
.32 centimeter	**10°** of arc
98.6° Fahrenheit	**60** acres

In ordinary text matter, fractions may be written out. However, where fractions and whole numbers appear together, use figures to express both numbers.

The stadium is about **three quarters** of a mile from the highway.
Give me a sheet of paper **8½** by **11** inches.
She ordered another box of **3½-by-5½-inch** cards.

If abbreviations or symbols are used for the unit of measure, the quantity should be expressed in figures.

3¾ mi.	6 V	35 mm film
25 MPH	32 g	30 cc
5″ by 7″	10%-15%	36°30′ N

Temperature
Temperature is expressed in figures with the degree sign plus the scale being used.

15° F (Fahrenheit)
−20° C (Celsius or centigrade)
12° K (Kelvin)

Parts of a Book
Generally, major book divisions are expressed in Roman numerals and minor divisions in Arabic figures. However, follow the style used in each book.

The material in **Part I, Chapters 6 through 8** covers how to refinance your house.

Plates, figures, tables, pages, and so on are also set in Arabic figures. The only general exception to this rule occurs in the preliminary or introductory pages of a book, which are usually set in Roman numerals.

Be sure to read pages **i-ix** before starting Chapter 1.
Plate **7** in Chapter **23** provides an excellent illustration of a genetic sequence.

I don't think figure **3.1** is accurate.
He has the final numbers for tables **2-4.**

Inclusive Numbers

Use the following guidelines for inclusive numbers. (The examples are page numbers, which do not require commas.)

1. For numbers less than 100, use all digits.

   4-23   86-92

2. For 100 or multiples of 100, use all digits.

   500-563

3. For 101 through 109 (and multiples of 100), use only the changed digits.

   101-4   503-6   1006-9

4. For 110 through 199 (and multiples of 100), use two digits or more as needed.

   112-24   467-68   1389-91   14285-389

Continued numbers other than pages are written in the following style:

the winter of **1980-81,** but the winter of **2000-2001** (when the
    century changes, use all four digits)
the years **1234-1345**
fiscal year **1984-85**
AD **712-14**
243-221 BC (All digits are used with BC years.)

When an inclusive date is used in a title, all digits are usually repeated.

*Brian Gregory's Journals: **1745-1789***
*World War II: **1939-1945***

Spelling and Word Division

To many writers, the English language seems riddled with exceptions to spelling rules. Yet most words conform to specific guidelines, and even the exceptions can be categorized for easy reference. The guidelines in this section explain how to spell most regular and many troublesome words. Appendix D provides a list of frequently misspelled words. Remember that the best guide to correct spelling is an up-to-date dictionary.

Spelling Guidelines

This section presents information specifically about dealing with prefixes, suffixes, and plurals. It also covers the rules for use of *i* and *e* combinations.

Prefixes

A *prefix* added at the beginning of a word changes its meaning. However, the prefix does not change the spelling of that word. Most prefixes are added without using a hyphen.

mis + step = misstep
im + memorial = immemorial
un + burden = unburden
over + enthusiastic = overenthusiastic
pre + formed = preformed
in + tolerable = intolerable
non + food = nonfood
re + draw = redraw

Exceptions: the prefixes *ex, self,* and *all* are always used with a hyphen when they are joined to nouns.

ex + prizefighter = ex-prizefighter
self + awareness = self-awareness
all + inclusive = all-inclusive

A hyphen is used when the prefix is joined to a proper noun or adjective.

non + English = non-English
pro + American = pro-American

A hyphen is used when the resulting word might be confused with a similar word of different meaning or when the word might be confusing to the eye.

re + creation = re-creation (not *recreation*)
re + emphasize = re-emphasize
sub + subheading = sub-subheading

Prefixes let us see how many words and terms English has borrowed from Greek, Latin, and French. Following is a list of the common prefixes used in English along with their meanings.

Old English

Prefix	Meaning	Example
a	in, on, of, up, to	arise, awake
be	around, about, away	behead, bedevil
for, fore	away, off, from	forsake, forewarn
mis	badly, poorly, not	misspell, mistake
over	above, excessively	overextend, oversee
un	not, reverse of	untidy, unnatural

Latin/
Latin-French

Prefix	Meaning	Example
ab, a, abs	from, off, away	absent, abscond
ante	before	antechamber, anteroom
bi	two	biweekly, bisect
circum	around	circumspect
col, com, con, co, cor	with, together	collide, companion, congregate, coexist, correlate
contra, contro	against	contradict, controversial
de	away, from, off, down	decline, depart
dif, dis	away, off, opposing	disagree, differ
e, ef, ex	away, from, out	efface, exit
im, in	in, into, within	immerse, include
il, im, in, ir	not	illegal, immoral, inescapable, irreverent
inter	among, between	intercept, interstate
intro, intra	inward, within	introduce, intrastate
non	not	nonclinical, nonessential
post	after, following	postscript, postoperative
pre	before	preceding, prevent
pro	forward, in place of, favoring	proceed, pronoun, pro-Canadian
re	back, backward, again	recede, recur, reduce
retro	back, backward	retroactive, retrojets
semi	half	semicircle, semimonthly
sub, suf, sum, sup, sus	under, beneath	suburb, suffuse, summon, support, suspicion
super	over, above, extra	supervise, superfluous
trans	across, beyond	transport, transnational
ultra	beyond, excessively	ultraviolet, ultramodern

Greek

Prefix	Meaning	Example
a	lacking, without	amoral, atheist
anti	against, opposing	antismoking, antithesis
apo	from, away	apology
cata	down, away, thoroughly	cataclysm, catacomb
dia	through, across, apart	diameter, dialogue
epi	at, on, over, among, beside	epidemic, epigraph
eu	good, pleasant	euphoria, eulogy
hemi	half	hemisphere
hyper	excessive, over	hyperactive, hypertension
hypo	under, beneath	hypodermic, hypotension
para	beside, beyond	parallel, paradox
peri	around	perimeter, peripheral
pro	before	prognosis, progress
syl, sym, syn, sys	together, with	syllable, sympathy, synthesis, systematic

Suffixes

A *suffix* is added to the end of the word. In many cases, the spelling of the word does not change.

sly + ly = slyly
awkward + ness = awkwardness
work + able = workable

The suffix *elect*, however, is always used with a hyphen.

secretary + elect = secretary-elect
president + elect = president-elect

There are several instances in which the spelling of the root word does change when a suffix is added. The following guidelines categorize these changes.

Final *y* as a Long *e* Sound. If the final *y* of a word represents a long *e* sound, then the final *y* changes to *i* before adding the suffix *ness* or *ly*.

merry + ly = merrily
dizzy + ness = dizziness

Final *y* Preceded by a Consonant. With words that end in *y* and are preceded by a consonant, change the *y* to *i* before any suffix not beginning with *i*.

sunny + er = sunnier
happy + ly = happily (but *hurry + ing = hurrying*)

Final *e* Before a Suffix Beginning with a Vowel. The final *e* is dropped before a suffix that begins with a vowel.

dare + ing = daring
sale + able = salable

The only exception to this rule is when the final *e* must be retained to maintain a soft *c* or *g* sound in the word.

notice + able = noticeable
courage + ous = courageous

Final *e* Before a Suffix Beginning with a Consonant. Keep the final *e* when adding a suffix that begins with a consonant.

use + ful = useful
care + less = careless

There are a few exceptions to this rule:

true + ly = truly (but *sincere + ly = sincerely*)
argue + ment = argument

Final *e* with the Suffix *ment*. When the final *e* in a word is preceded by two consonants, drop the final *e* and add the suffix.

acknowledge + ment = acknowledgment
judge + ment = judgment

When the final *e* in a word is preceded by a vowel and a consonant, keep the final *e* and add the suffix.

manage + ment = management

Double Final Consonant Before a Suffix Beginning with a Vowel. The final consonant of a word is doubled when (1) the word has only one syllable, (2) the accent falls on the last syllable of the word (*prefer*), or (3) the word ends in a single consonant preceded by a single vowel.

drag + ed = dragged
sit + ing = sitting
omit + ing = omitting
ocCUR + ed = occurred
preFER + ing = preferring (but *PREferable*)
conTROL + able = controllable

Single Final Consonant Before a Suffix. The final consonant remains single if the word is accented on the first syllable; if the final consonant is already double it remains double.

TARget + ed = targeted
CANcel + ing = canceling
tell + ing = telling
pull + ed = pulled

Words Ending in a Hard *c* Sound. For words ending in a hard *c* sound, add *k* before suffixes *in, ed,* and *y.*

panic + y = panicky
picnic + ing = picnicking
traffic + ed = trafficked
mimic + ing = mimicking

Suffixes *sede, ceed,* and *cede*. Only one word in English ends in *sede*.

super + sede = supersede

Only three words in English end in *ceed*.

exceed   proceed   succeed

All other words with similar sounds end in *cede*.

precede   recede   secede   concede   accede

Suffixes *able* and *ible*. The suffixes *able* and *ible* sound alike and mean nearly the same things such as "capable of being" and "worthy of being." They are added to verbs and nouns to form adjectives.

irritate + able = irritable
permission + ible = permissible

There is a handy rule of thumb for knowing when to use *able* or *ible* that works for most words. When a related word can be formed ending in *ation*, then *able* is the correct suffix. When a related word can be formed ending in *ion* or *ive*, then *ible* is correct.

dur*ation* = dur*able*
irrit*ation* = irrit*able*
repress*ion* = repress*ible*
permiss*ive* = permiss*ible*

If a word is not in the dictionary, it is spelled with *able*.
When the suffix *able* is added to a word ending in *e*, the final *e* is dropped unless preceded by a *c* or *g*.

desire + able = desirable
use + able = usable
notice + able = noticeable
knowledge + able = knowledgeable

Suffixes *ant* and *ent*, *ance* and *ence*. The four suffixes *ant, ent, ance,* and *ence* are added to change verbs to nouns and adjectives.

    attend + ant = attendant
    insist + ent = insistent
    attend + ance = attendance
    insist + ence = insistence

Unfortunately, there is no rule for knowing when to use which suffix. Memorize the spellings of words with these endings. However, if the word you wish to spell is not in the dictionary, use *ant* or *ance*.

Suffixes *er* and *or*. The suffixes *er* and *or* sound alike and both mean *one who*. Some words are spelled with either ending.

    act + or = actor   advise + or = advisor
    drive + er = driver   advise + er = adviser
    visit + or = visitor   speak + er = speaker

The suffix *er* is more common and is added to all new words in English. The suffix *or* occurs mainly with Latin root words, particularly legal terms, and is no longer added to words in English. If a word cannot be found in the dictionary, use the *er* suffix.

Suffixes *ize* and *ise*. The suffixes *ize* and *ise* are added to adjectives and nouns to make verbs. The suffix *ize* is used in American English while the suffix *ise* is British.

    legal + ize = legalize
    custom + ize = customize
    critic + ize = criticize

Some words use either suffix as an ending, while others are spelled only with *ise*.

mesmer + ise = mesmerise
mesmer + ize = mesmerize

advise   exercise   enterprise   disguise   chastise

If a word is not in the dictionary, use the *ize* suffix as the correct ending.

Suffixes, like prefixes, have been added to English from several sources. Following is a list of the most common suffixes for nouns, adjectives, and verbs from Old English, Greek, Latin, and French along with their meanings.

Old English

Noun Suffixes	Meaning	Example
dom	state, rank, condition	kingdom, wisdom, martyrdom
er	doer, maker	writer, teacher
hood	state, condition	statehood, brotherhood
ness	quality, state	hardness, likeness

Latin, French, Greek Noun

Suffixes	Meaning	Example
age	process, state, rank	peerage, passage
ance, ancy	act, condition, fact	vigilance, vacancy
ard, art	one that does (in excess)	coward, braggart
ate	office, rank	delegate, potentate
ation	action, state, result	occupation, starvation
cy	state, condition	delinquency, accuracy
ee	one receiving action	retiree, employee
eer	doer, worker at	engineer, mountaineer
ence	act, condition, fact	evidence, sentence
er	doer, native of	financier, baker
ery	skill, action, collection	surgery, cookery
ess	feminine	princess, lioness
et, ette	little, feminine	islet, majorette

Latin, French, Greek Noun Suffixes

Suffixes	Meaning	Example
ion	action, result, state	union, conclusion
ism	act, manner, doctrine	baptism, barbarism, feminism
ist	doer, believer	plagiarist, socialist
ition	action, state, result	sedition, expedition
ity	state, quality, condition	civility, rarity
ment	means, result, action	embarrassment, fulfillment
or	doer, office, action	actor, juror
ry	condition, practice, collection	archery, jewelry
tion	action, condition	delegation, destruction
tude	quality, state, result	multitude, fortitude
ty	quality, state	witty, beauty
ure	act, result, means	culture, ligature
y	result, action, quality	arty, jealousy, handy

Old English Adjective Suffixes

Suffixes	Meaning	Example
en	made of, like	silken, golden
ful	full of, marked by	thoughtful, careful
ish	suggesting, like	prudish, childish
less	lacking, without	thankless, hopeless
like	like, similar	catlike, dreamlike
ly	like, of the nature of	heavily, friendly
some	apt to, showing	worrisome, tiresome
ward	in the direction of	forward, downward
y	showing, suggesting	heavy, wavy, rocky

Foreign
Adjective

Suffixes	Meaning	Example
able	able, likely	workable, likeable
ate	having, showing	animate, duplicate
escent	becoming, growing	obsolescent
esque	in the style of, like	statuesque, picturesque
fic	making, causing	terrific
ible	able, likely, fit	producible, edible
ose	marked by, given to	bellicose, comatose
ous	marked by, given to	wondrous, religious

Foreign
Adjective/Noun

Suffixes	Meaning	Example
al	doer, pertaining to	ritual, autumnal
an	one belonging to, pertaining to	American, human
ant	actor, agent, showing	servant
ary	belonging to, one connected with	functionary, adversary
ent	doing, showing, actor	agent, confident
ese	of a place or style	Japanese, journalese
ian	pertaining to, one belonging to	reptilian, Sicilian
ic	dealing with, caused by, person or thing	scientific, epidemic
ile	marked by, one marked by	senile, juvenile
ine	marked by, dealing with, one marked by	divine, feline, marine
ite	formed, showing, one marked by	Muscovite, favorite, composite
ory	doing, pertaining to, place or thing for	accessory, observatory

Old English

Verb Suffix	Meaning	Example
en	cause to be, become	enliven, awaken

Foreign

Verb Suffixes	Meaning	Example
ate	become, form, treat	formulate, agitate
esce	become, grow, continue	convalesce, acquiesce
fy	make, cause, cause to harm	fortify, glorify
ish	do, make, perform	finish, distinguish
ize	make, cause to be	mobilize, sterilize

Plurals

We have already briefly touched on plurals of words; here is more detailed information.

Regular Nouns. The plural of most nouns is formed by adding *s*.

Singular	Plural
eagle	eagles
minister	ministers
record	records

Irregular Nouns. For most irregular nouns, the spelling changes to form the plural. Because the spelling changes do not follow any general rule, the forms must be memorized.

Singular	Plural
child	children
goose	geese
man	men
mouse	mice
woman	women

Some irregular nouns keep the same form for both singular and plural.

Singular	Plural
deer	deer
sheep	sheep
species	species

Nouns Ending in *s, ss, z, sh, ch,* and *x*. For nouns ending in *s, ss, z, sh, ch,* and *x,* add *es* to form the plural.

Singular	Plural
address	addresses
box	boxes
buzz	buzzes
dish	dishes
fez	fezes
gas	gases
kiss	kisses
watch	watches

Nouns Ending in *y*. For nouns ending in *y* preceded by a consonant, change the *y* to *i* and add *es*. For nouns ending in *y* preceded by a vowel, simply add *s*.

NOUNS ENDING IN *Y* PRECEDED BY A CONSONANT

Singular	Plural
category	categories
currency	currencies
secretary	secretaries
territory	territories

NOUNS ENDING IN *Y* PRECEDED BY A VOWEL

Singular	Plural
delay	delays
holiday	holidays
relay	relays
Wednesday	Wednesdays

Nouns Ending in *o*. For nouns ending in *o* preceded by a consonant, add *s* or *es*. If the *o* is preceded by a vowel, add *s*.

NOUNS ENDING IN *O* PRECEDED BY A CONSONANT

Singular	Plural
hero	heroes
potato	potatoes
solo	solos
tomato	tomatoes
zero	zeroes

NOUNS ENDING IN *O* PRECEDED BY A VOWEL

Singular	Plural
radio	radios
stereo	stereos
studio	studios

All musical and literary terms ending in *o* add *s* to form the plural.

Singular	Plural
oratorio	oratorios
piano	pianos
rondo	rondos
soprano	sopranos

Nouns ending in *f* or *fe*. Many nouns ending in *f* or *fe* simply add *s* to form the plural. However, some nouns change the *f* to *v* and add *es*.

ADD *S*

Singular	Plural
chief	chiefs
dwarf	dwarfs

CHANGE *F* OR *FE* TO *V* AND ADD *ES*

Singular	Plural
half	halves
knife	knives
life	lives
self	selves
wife	wives
wolf	wolves

Compound Nouns as One Word. Compound nouns written as one word and ending in *s, sh, ch,* or *x* form the plural by adding *es*. In all other cases, the plural is formed by simply adding *s*.

COMPOUND NOUNS ADDING *ES*

Singular	Plural
lockbox	lockboxes
toothbrush	toothbrushes

COMPOUND NOUNS ADDING *S*

Singular	Plural
firefighter	firefighters
mainframe	mainframes

Compound Nouns as Two Words. The plural of compound nouns written as two or more words is formed by making the main word plural.

Singular	Plural
chairman of the board	chairmen of the board
editor in chief	editors in chief
notary public	notary publics *or* notaries public
vice president	vice presidents

Hyphenated Compound Nouns. Hyphenated compound nouns are made plural either by adding *s* to the main word or, if there is no main word, adding *s* to the end of the compound.

ADDING *S* TO THE MAIN WORD

Singular	Plural
ex-governor	ex-governors
passer-by	passers-by
president-elect	presidents-elect
son-in-law	sons-in-law

ADDING *S* TO THE END OF THE COMPOUND

Singular	Plural
grown-up	grown-ups
start-up	start-ups
trade-in	trade-ins
write-in	write-ins

Foreign Words. Some foreign words form plurals as they would in the original language.

Singular	Plural
alumna (female)	alumnae
alumnus (male)	alumni
basis	bases
crisis	crises
datum	data
tableau	tableaux

Other foreign words form the plural either as they do in the original language or by adding *s* or *es* as in English. When in doubt about the preferred form, consult a dictionary.

Singular	Foreign Plural	English Plural
appendix	appendices	appendixes
formula	formulae	formulas
index	indices	indexes

Numbers, Letters, Words, Symbols. The plural of numbers, letters, words, and symbols is formed by adding *'s* to the term.

three 5's	two &'s and three #'s
use l's and m's	yes's and no's

The i *and* e *Rules*

Use *i* before *e*, except after *c*, for the long *e* sound in a word.

believe	relieve
grievance	retrieve
piece	thief

The exceptions to this rule are the words *either, neither, leisure, seized,* and *weird.*

Use *e* before *i* after *c* for the long *e* sound in a word.

ceiling	receipt
deceive	receive

Use *e* before *i* when the sound in the word is not long *e.*

eight	neighbor
freight	weigh
height	weight

Word Division

Like spelling rules, the rules for word division may seem arbitrary. Actually, they follow specific guidelines. The following rules explain the basics of properly dividing words. A good dictionary is the best guide for dividing words correctly.

General Rules

Following are two general rules for word division.

1. Avoid dividing words at the end of more than three successive lines.

   Avoid: We came into the conference hall late but man-
   aged to find our seat-
   ing arrangements before
   the first speaker began.

   Better: We came into the conference hall late but man-
   aged to find our seating
   arrangements before the
   first speaker began.

2. Avoid dividing a word at the end of a page or dividing the last word of a paragraph.

Syllables and Word Division

Words are divided only between syllables. As a result, one-syllable words such as *trough, while,* and *there* are never divided.

Each syllable in word division must contain a vowel; therefore, most contractions cannot be divided.

con-trol (not *con-tr-ol*)   couldn't (not *could-n't*)
hy-drau-lic (not *hy-dr-au-lic*) isn't (not *is-n't*)

When a word is divided, there must be more than one letter on the first line and more than two letters on the second line.

Incorrect:	He apologized to everyone most **sincere-ly.**
Correct:	He apologized to everyone most **sin-cerely.**
Incorrect:	She told reporters that all her **jewel-ry** had been stolen.
Correct:	She told reporters that all her **jew-elry** had been stolen.
Incorrect:	"Look at this letter; it's full of **e-rasures.**"
Correct:	"Look at this letter; it's full of **era-sures.**"
Incorrect:	He's not sick. He's suffering from **a-pathy.**
Correct:	He's not sick. He's suffering from **ap-athy.**

Single-Letter Syllables

A single-letter syllable will always be a vowel. Generally, a single-letter syllable within a word should be left with the first part of the word and not carried over to the second line.

bus-i-ness = busi-ness (not *bus-iness*)
ox-y-gen = oxy-gen (not *ox-ygen*)
sep-a-rate = sepa-rate (not *sep-arate*)

When two single-letter syllables occur together in a word, divide the word between the single-letter syllables.

grad-u-a-tion = gradu-ation (not *grad-uation*)
in-sin-u-a-tion = insinu-ation (not *insin-uation*)

When the single-letter syllable *a, i,* or *u* is followed by the final syllable *ble, bly,* or *cal,* join the two end syllables and carry them over to the next line.

cler-i-cal = cler-ical (not *cleri-cal*)
de-pend-a-ble = depend-able (not *dependa-ble*)

Final and Double Consonants

If a final consonant preceded by a vowel is doubled before adding a suffix, divide the word between the two consonants.

plan + ing = planning = plan-ning
set + ing = setting = set-ting
win + ing = winning = win-ning

If the root word ends in a double consonant before the suffix is added, divide the word between the root word and the suffix.

assess + ing = assessing = assess-ing
tell + ing = telling = tell-ing

A word should never be divided between two or three consonants pronounced as one.

catch-ing (not *cat-ching*)
cush-ion (not *cus-hion*)
leath-ery (not *leat-hery*)

Hyphenated Words

Divide hyphenated words and compound hyphenated words only at the hyphen that connects them.

self-assessment = self-assessment (not *self-assess-ment*)
ex-husband = ex-husband (not *ex-hus-band*)
client-oriented approach = client-oriented approach (not
client-or-iented approach)

Proper Names

Avoid dividing a person's name or any proper name. Separate titles, initials, or degrees from names only when it is unavoidable.

Avoid:	Mrs. Joan Cunning- ham
Better:	Mrs. Joan Cunningham
Avoid:	Ms. Angela Sortino
Better:	Ms. Angela Sortino
Avoid:	George Watson, PhD
Better:	George Watson, PhD

Figures and Abbreviations

In general, avoid dividing figures and abbreviations. However, if parts of an address or date must be separated, use the following guidelines.

Dividing Addresses

Avoid:	15 Water Street
Better:	15 Water Street
Avoid:	557 West Lock- port
Better:	557 West Lockport
Avoid:	1903 71st Avenue

Better: 1903 71st
Avenue

Avoid: New York, New
York

Better: New York,
New York

Dividing Dates

Avoid: August
20, 1976

Better: August 20,
1976

Avoid: September 15, 19-
55

Better: September 15,
1955

PART II

Style Considerations

Although style in writing is a highly individual matter, some general rules and guidelines have been developed over the years to produce more precise, lively, and informative prose. This part discusses sentence structure and patterns; brevity, clarity, and accuracy; and gender-inclusive language.

Sentences

In composing sentences, many writers end up with one of two extremes: short, choppy sentences or long, complex ones. Thoughts may be expressed in brief, staccato statements that leave the reader short of breath. Or a sentence may start out with one idea and add a qualifier here, a modifier there, and an incidental fact or two. By the time the sentence is finished, it has become a verbal maze for the reader.

Writing clear, informative sentences is as much art as it is the skilled use of grammatical rules. The guidelines presented in this section explain how to compose sentences that convey the intended meaning and capture the reader's interest.

The following guidelines show how to use various sentence patterns to express ideas.

Use Clarity and Meaning as the Criteria for Good Sentences

Each sentence should say *something* about the central idea of its paragraph without saying *too much or too little*. Build the reader's understanding key step by key step. In the following example, the writer has presented the facts in undersized bites, creating an awkward style.

Choppy: Hank sailed around the world. He did it alone in a thirty-foot sailboat. His radio was his only link with the outside world. He caught fish for his meals and trapped rainwater to drink. His solitary journey took 168 days.

In the second example, the writer has committed the opposite fault of trying to say everything in one sentence.

Run-On: Hank sailed around the world in 168 days in a thirty-foot sailboat with only a radio to connect him to the outside world and only fresh fish and rainwater to keep his provisions stocked.

Both examples express complete thoughts, but the clarity and meaning of the information is muddled by the way it is presented. What facts in the story are more important than the others? Is there some way of ordering the material so the reader has a sense of key facts versus merely interesting ones?

In the following revision, the writer has ordered the information and used clarity and meaning as the criteria for sentence construction.

Revised: Hank completed his record solo voyage around the world in a mere 168 days. He made the journey in a thirty-foot sailboat, whose shortwave radio served as his only link with the outside world. He kept his provisions stocked by catching fish and trapping rainwater to drink.

In the revised version, the reader is given not only the necessary information but also some idea of its importance and meaning.

Include Only One to Two Ideas in Each Sentence

Many times writers will trap themselves into long, involved sentences because they are free-associating rather than carefully constructing their thoughts. A series of ideas in one sentence rushes the reader too quickly through the material. Before one idea has time to settle, another crowds it out of the way. Such sentences can be separated into shorter, simpler constructions.

Original: Our study on the impact of the Environmental Pollution Act revealed that water quality has improved by an average of 35 percent in 14 states but toxic waste is still a major concern among most residents because this issue has not been addressed in any systematic way because of confusion within the Environmental Protection Agency about how to enforce the regulations.

Conjunctions such as *and, but,* and *because* often signal where a new sentence can begin. The preceding paragraph can be rewritten as follows:

Revised: Our study on the impact of the Environmental Pollution Act revealed that water quality has improved by an average of 35 percent in 14 states. Toxic waste, however, is still a major concern among most residents. This issue has not been addressed systematically because the Environmental Protection Agency has not set guidelines on enforcing toxic waste regulations.

In the revision, each sentence contains only one or two ideas. The reader has time to absorb the information in each sentence before going on to the next one.

Vary Sentence Patterns to Avoid Monotonous Use of Any Particular Construction

A writer may unconsciously adopt one type of sentence pattern throughout a paragraph. A short, staccato pattern can mimic a cool, unemotional tone. On the other hand, if all the sentences begin with subordinate clauses, it may appear that the paragraph is taking a circular route to the main point.

The English sentence can be composed in a variety of ways to add interest and liveliness. The four basic sentence constructions—simple, compound, complex, and compound-complex—can be combined in paragraphs to help the reader move from one idea to the next.

Let's review the four basic sentence patterns:

Simple:	I would like to go home. (an independent clause with no subordinate clause)
Compound:	I'm not feeling well, and I would like to go home. (two or more independent clauses but no subordinate clause)
Complex:	Because I'm not feeling well, I would like to go home. (an independent clause and one or more subordinate clauses)
Compound-complex:	I'm not feeling well because I ate six taffy apples, and I would like to go home. (two or more independent clauses and one or more subordinate clauses—underscored)

The following example is written exclusively in short, simple sentences. The revision uses complex and compound sentences to vary the constructions. Read the two versions aloud. Notice how the change in rhythm affects the reader's perception and feelings about the material.

Monotonous:	Bond entered Mecca through the south gate. The sun was high overhead. Its brutal heat struck him speechless. Pilgrims blocked the narrow streets and alleyways. His guide found him lodgings near the mosque. He would be contacted soon by the Mecca agent. He had only two days left to complete his mission.
Varied:	Bond entered Mecca through the south gate. The sun was high overhead, and its brutal heat struck him speechless. In every section of the city, pilgrims blocked the narrow streets and alleyways. His guide found him lodgings near the mosque, and Bond settled in to wait for the Mecca agent. With only two days left to complete his mission, Bond hoped the man would arrive soon.

In the next example, the writer uses introductory subordinate clauses for all sentences. Read aloud the two versions and notice how varying the sentence structure changes the rhythm and tone of the text.

Monotonous:	After waiting 24 hours, Bond knew that something was wrong. Because he had used only embassy couriers to carry his messages, he suspected a security leak among the embassy staff. Even if his suspicions were wrong, it was evident that somewhere along the line the message had been intercepted. Although his orders said to stay in Mecca, Bond left the city that night.
Varied:	After waiting 24 hours, Bond knew that something was wrong. He had used only embassy couriers to carry his messages to the Mecca contact. Was there a security leak among the embassy staff? His suspicions might be groundless, but somewhere along the line the message had been intercepted. Although his orders said to stay in Mecca, Bond left the city that night.

Experiment with various sentence patterns by recasting sentences in the four basic forms. Use the following examples as guides for rewriting sentences. Notice that by altering the patterns, different facts in the sentence can be stressed.

Simple:	He reached Akaba and learned the Mecca agent had disappeared.
Compound:	He reached Akaba, and headquarters told him the Mecca agent had disappeared.
Complex:	When he reached Akaba, headquarters told him the Mecca agent had disappeared.
Compound-complex:	By the time Bond reached Akaba, the Mecca agent had disappeared, and all the agent's contacts had been arrested.

Brevity

Brevity means "brief" or "concise." It has been said that "brevity is the soul of wit." Many sentences are inflated with wordy phrases or expressions that add nothing to the meaning or impact of what is being said. The following guidelines explain how to make written messages more concise.

Avoid the Phrases *There Is* and *There Are*
Rewrite sentences using more active verbs.

Avoid: There are three reasons for colonizing Mars.
Better: I can tell you three reasons for colonizing Mars.
Three reasons exist for colonizing Mars.
Avoid: Whenever it rains, there is water in our backyard.
Better: Whenever it rains, water collects in our backyard.
Whenever it rains, our backyard floods.

Condense Clauses Beginning with *Which, That,* or *Who* into Fewer Words
Rewriting clauses beginning with *which, that,* or *who* will often eliminate wordy phrases.

Poor: The visitor, who was from England, brought us a package that looked mysterious.
Better: The English visitor brought us a mysterious package.

Poor: The building, which was 24 stories, collapsed during the
         earthquake that struck last night.
Better: The 24-story building collapsed during last night's
         earthquake.

Strike Out the Article *the* Wherever Possible

Eliminating *the* will improve the flow and readability of sentences. The importance of *the* can be determined by crossing it out and reading the sentence for meaning. If the sentence is less clear, restore the article.

~~The~~ shore lights reflected in Santiago Bay made the hotels and ~~the~~ casinos appear to float above the water.

~~The~~ players compete in ~~the~~ spring for the starting positions that ~~the~~ management has posted.

Eliminate Wordy and Redundant Phrases and Expressions

Redundant words and expressions repeat or rephrase what has been said in a sentence. They occur frequently in writing and should be deleted. Here are a few examples.

Avoid: The blouse is bright yellow **in color**.
Better: The blouse is bright yellow.
Avoid: Of course, we're only thinking **on a theoretical basis**.
Better: Of course, we're only thinking theoretically.
Avoid: **In the vast majority of cases**, chicken pox is not fatal.
Better: In most cases, chicken pox is not fatal.
Avoid: **The reason** I don't want you to go is **that** the Amazon is no
         place for a summer vacation.
Better: I don't want you to go because the Amazon is no place for a
         summer vacation.

Following is a list of wordy phrases commonly used by many writers. Compare them with their more concise alternatives. Change the wordy phrases wherever they appear.

Wordy	Concise
at this point in time	at this time
consensus of opinion	consensus
meet together	meet
blend together	blend
during the course of	during
few in number	few
personal in manner	personal
on a weekly basis	weekly
refer back to	refer to
square in shape	square
until such time as	until
due to the fact that	because
very necessary	necessary
in spite of the fact that	although
engaged in a study of	studying
depreciate in value	depreciate
opening gambit	gambit (a gambit is an opening move in chess)
this is a subject that	this subject
the fact that she had come	her coming
in a hasty manner	hastily

Redundant expressions are easy to spot once you learn how and where to look for them.

Avoid: To find his error, he had to retrace the steps **he had taken before**. (*Retrace* means to go back over the steps or path taken before. The clause in boldface is unnecessary.)

Better: To find his error, he had to retrace his steps.

Avoid: In **the month of** June, we traveled through **the states of** Georgia, North Carolina, and Virginia.

Better: In June, we traveled through Georgia, North Carolina, and Virginia.

8

Clarity

Clear writing involves getting the words just right. Choose the best words to express your ideas in the best manner possible. Do not assume that written material is clear to the reader. This section presents guidelines for clear writing.

Keep Words Fresh

Writing should be free of jargon, buzzwords, and clichés. Such words and phrases come easily to mind yet convey little real information. Delete them and substitute more precise words.

Jargon

Jargon refers to specialized terms of a profession that the general reader probably would not understand. Rewrite sentences to eliminate jargon or make sure that all terms are defined.

Avoid: Doctors often order tests to check patients' **mineral spectrums** and the **RBC counts** in their blood.

Better: Doctors often order tests to check patients' **trace minerals, such as iron,** and the **number of red blood cells** in their blood.

Buzzwords

Buzzwords are terms that come into fashion for a time and find their way into everyone's writing. They are often borrowed from various professions and adapted to general use. Eliminate buzzwords and choose better words. Some of today's buzzwords include the following:

amp it up	interactive	head honcho
input	bottom line	parameter
paradigm	interface	dicey
scenario	street smarts	at this point in time
viable	taxwise (or anything *wise*)	impact (as a verb)

Avoid: I don't know how well Greg is going to **interface** with Linda. They haven't worked together before.

Better: I don't know how well Greg is going to **get along with** Linda. They haven't worked together before.

Some words and phrases from the legal field have been appropriated for general use—often inappropriately. Avoid using the following terms for everyday writing:

aforementioned	per, as per
duly	pursuant to
herein	therein
hereto	therewith
herewith	whereas
notwithstanding the above	

Avoid: **Re** your letter of the 25th, we are sending your five memo pads **per** your order and enclosing the invoice **herein**. (Not only do the "legal" terms add nothing to the sentence, but the writer misses a chance to communicate more precise details.)

Better: We received your order, dated October 25, for five memo pads. Enclosed please find the memo pads and an invoice itemizing price and shipping costs.

Clichés

Clichés are trite, worn-out expressions. While they are acceptable in conversation, they should be avoided in writing. Following are some common clichés:

stiff as a board	slick as a whistle
oldies but goodies	keep your shirt on
mind-blowing	too good to be true
crying over spilt milk	getting in touch with
on the warpath	out of the frying pan
up to your ears	on the tip of my tongue
deader than a doornail	bigger than life
neat as a pin	needle in a haystack
pearls of wisdom	a stitch in time

Avoid: The boss is **on the warpath** about the new product failure. I thought the sales projections were **too good to be true**. Now we're **up to our ears** in returned goods.

Better: The boss is **demanding to know why** the new product failed. I thought the sales projections were **too optimistic**. Now we have **more than 100,000 units** of returned goods.

Keep Words Specific and Concrete

The more abstract a word or phrase, the less people will understand exactly what is meant. Abstract terms are subject to considerable individual interpretation. For example, the terms *national security, quality education,* and *consumer interests* can mean widely different things to different people.

Concrete words, on the other hand, refer to something specific, often something that can be seen, heard, touched, tasted, or smelled. Their meaning is also more precise and less open to personal interpretation. Use concrete words as much as possible in writing. Although abstract words can be used for summarizing ideas and creating a framework for discussion, ground the framework in tangible, concrete details.

Abstract: I think this novel is **overly dramatic.**
Concrete: I think this novel relies too much on emotion, coincidence, and manipulation of characters.
Abstract: The company's sales picture is **gloomy** this year.
Concrete: The 25 percent drop in sales means we will probably not meet our objectives this year.
Abstract: His tennis game is **off.**
Concrete: His backstroke is weak, and he can't maintain his concentration.

Many people also try to make their writing sound more formal or official by using abstract words instead of concrete ones.

Avoid: Please refrain from discarding litter items on the company grounds or in the company buildings. Use the litter receptacles placed throughout the plant for such purposes. Your cooperation in this matter is appreciated.
Better: Please deposit all waste paper, aluminum cans, bottles, and other trash in the appropriate litter baskets. Help keep your grounds and building clean! We appreciate your cooperation.

Vague or abstract words leave unanswered such questions as *What kind? How much? Which one? In what way?* By using concrete words, readers' questions are answered with specific information.

Keep References Clear

When words are used to modify or refer to other words, make sure the reader can follow the intended train of thought. If references are used carelessly, some unintended humor may be provided.

If you can't hang the clothes yourself, ask for help in hanging them from your counselor.
Our camp leader is a stocky, red-haired man with a beach ball named Tom Robbins.

Such confusion can be avoided by following a few basic guidelines to keep references clear.

Keep Modifiers Close to Words They Modify

Poor: The band played **three songs** during their tour **written by a 12-year-old girl**.

Better: During their tour, the band played **three songs written by a 12-year-old girl**.

Place Adverbs Close to Words They Modify

Pay particular attention to placement of the adverb *only*. The reader should not have to guess at the sentence's meaning.

Incorrect: I **only** wanted three lattes, not five.

Correct: I wanted **only** three lattes, not five.

Poor: The letter we **received recently managed** to upset everyone. (Is it *received recently* or *recently managed?*)

Better: The letter we **recently received managed** to upset everyone.

Keep Subject and Verb Together

This arrangement helps the reader follow the thought and understand the sentence more easily.

Avoid: **The white-pebble beach,** which in June 1944 had been the site of a bloody battle where the Allied forces landed and began their march to liberate Europe from German occupation, **still bears the scars of a major military campaign.**

Better: **The white-pebble beach still bears the scars of a major military campaign.** In June 1944 it was the site of a bloody battle where the Allied forces landed and began their march to liberate Europe from German occupation.

Often the solution to the problem of subject-verb placement is to break the sentence into two or more shorter sentences.

Make Sure That Antecedents Are Clear

Words such as *this, that, who, what, which,* and *it* refer to the preceding noun or pronoun in the sentence or previous sentence. If the antecedents are not clear, the sentences will confuse the reader and may provide some unexpected humor.

> We will paint any car, any make, for only $59.95. Our offer is good for this week only. Have your car painted before it expires!

The antecedent for *it* is *our offer*, not *your car*. But the reader must look twice at the sentence to determine the writer's true intention. Study the following examples.

Poor: I served avocados for lunch, **which** no one felt like eating. (Did no one feel like eating the avocados or the lunch?)

Better: I served avocados for lunch, but no one felt like eating them. No one felt like eating the avocados I served for lunch.

Poor: I dropped the jar and pickles rolled all over the floor, under the table, and out into the hallway. **This** was not going to please my mother! (To what does *this* refer? Avoid using words that refer to an entire sentence or idea.)

Better: I dropped the jar and pickles rolled all over the floor, under the table, and out into the hallway. **This mess** was not going to please my mother!

A variety of methods can be used to correct confusing references. These include breaking one sentence into two or more, rearranging word order, restating the sentence, or filling in the missing reference.

Keep Structures Parallel

Phrases and clauses in a series or within a sentence should be parallel; that is, they should have the same structure. In the following example, the writer begins with infinitive phrases and then changes to another structure at the end.

> We learned how to change a tire, to shift 16 gears, and once stopped the truck from running off the road.

Once a parallel structure has been started, the reader expects it to continue. If the structure changes in midstream, readers will be confused. The preceding example should read as follows:

> We learned how **to change** a tire, **to shift** 16 gears, and **to stop** the truck from running off the road.

Look over the following examples. In some cases, the violation of parallel structure is not obvious.

Incorrect:	We sold jeans to **the** Spanish, **the** French, Italians, and Germans.
Correct:	We sold jeans to **the** Spanish, **the** French, **the** Italians, and **the** Germans.
	We sold jeans to **the** Spanish, French, Italians, and Germans.

An article or preposition used in a series of terms must be used with all the terms or only before the first term.

Correlative conjunctions—such as *both, and*; *not, but*; *not only, but also*; and *either, or*—should be followed by the same grammatical structure. This rule is also true for any series introduced by *first, second, third,* and so on. The sentence may need to be rearranged to correct the problem.

Incorrect:	The lecture was **both a tedious one and much too long**.
Correct:	The lecture was **both tedious and long**.

Incorrect:	It's not a time **for emotion but clear thinking.**
Correct:	It's not a time **for** emotion **but for** clear thinking.
Incorrect:	My reasons are **first,** the expedition is too dangerous and **second, that it is unnecessary.**
Correct:	My reasons are **first,** the expedition is too dangerous and **second, it is unnecessary.**

Writers also violate parallel structure when they mix verb forms within a sentence.

I have mowed the lawn, **washed** the dog, **rescued** our hamster, and **went** to the store all in one day.

The verb form *went* is incorrect with the auxiliary verb *have*. The sentence can be rewritten as follows:

I **have mowed** the lawn, **washed** the dog, **rescued** our hamster, and **gone** to the store all in one day.
I **mowed** the lawn, **washed** the dog, **rescued** our hamster, and **went** to the store all in one day.

Accuracy

Accuracy is essential to good writing, whether the writing is an essay, a business report, a term paper, or a news article. The following guidelines help ensure that facts are correct.

Double-Check Figures, Dates, Specifications, and Other Details

The motto is *When in doubt, check it out*. Make sure that any figures, dates, percentages, or other facts have been reported or copied accurately. Do not rely on memory.

Be Sure That All Names, Titles, and Abbreviations Are Spelled Properly

It can be considerably embarrassing to misspell proper names and titles of books, articles, plays, and the like. Find out whether abbreviations are spelled with periods, in all capitals, or with symbols such as ampersands.

Verify the Accuracy of Direct Quotations

Try to verify what people said and report their words accurately. In one instance, a reporter asked a political candidate the following question: "Do you believe that we should do away with price supports for farmers and import more foreign commodities?"

The candidate replied, "Yes," and the reporter wrote in an article:

Candidate Brown said, "We should do away with price supports for farmers and import more foreign commodities."

The candidate said nothing of the kind; he merely responded to a question. The reporter should have written the following:

When asked if he favors eliminating price supports and importing more foreign commodities, the candidate replied, "Yes."

Make Sure That Ideas Are Presented Clearly

Clarity is essential to accuracy. Learn to spot muddled statements, abstract terms, nonparallel constructions, ambiguous expressions, and poor development of ideas.

Ask someone else to read what you have written. Chances are he or she will be able to point out weaknesses in your work that you cannot see.

Make Sure Your Work Is Neat and Legible

Sloppy handwriting, messy copy, or spelling and grammatical errors can affect the accuracy of your work. Someone's name may be misspelled because you could not read your own handwriting. A key figure may be blurred by a coffee stain, and you will have to search through your notes to find the correct number. Carelessness not only threatens accuracy but also can cost you considerable time and effort.

Gender-Inclusive Language

Use of gender-biased language can create confusion. For example, the use of the word *man* sometimes refers only to men and other times refers to both men and women. The conversion from sexist to gender-inclusive language can be made naturally and gracefully. In the following sections, guidelines are provided for using gender-inclusive nouns, pronouns, titles, and expressions.

Nouns and Pronouns

Here are guidelines for the use of gender-inclusive and the avoidance of gender-specific nouns and pronouns.

1. Try to use female and male pronouns only when referring to specific males and females.

    Avoid: A good dentist reassures **his** patients.
    Better: Dr. Jacobs always reassures **his** patients.
    Dr. Jacobs always reassures **her** patients.
    Avoid: An elementary teacher has **her** hands full teaching today's children.
    Better: Ms. Hutton has **her** hands full teaching today's children.
    Mr. Hutton has **his** hands full teaching today's children.

Note: on occasion, use male and female paired pronouns *he or she, her or him, his or hers,* etc., instead of a male or female pronoun exclusively. This construction is particularly appropriate as a gentle reminder that both men and women make up the population that is being discussed.

Avoid:	A good manager knows **his** staff.
Better:	A good manager knows **his or her** staff.

2. Make the nouns and pronouns plural.

Avoid:	The prudent **executive** should know where **his** money goes.
Better:	Prudent **executives** should know where **their** money goes.
Avoid:	The course is designed to help **your child** reach **her** full potential.
Better:	The course is designed to help **children** reach **their** full potential.

Note: in informal writing and speech it is permissible to use the plural pronouns *they, them, their,* and *theirs* with a singular noun or indefinite pronoun. However, you can usually recast the sentence to avoid this construction.

Avoid:	Each manager knows **his** staff.
(Sometimes) Better:	Each manager knows **their** staff.

3. Use the first-person *we,* second-person *you,* or third-person *one, each, those,* and so on, where appropriate.

Avoid:	**Man's** desire for excitement drives **him** to seek ever more daring challenges.
Better:	**Our** desire for excitement drives **us** to seek ever more daring challenges.
Avoid:	The **player** cannot throw the dice until **he** has drawn one card from the Community Chest pile.
Better:	**You** cannot throw the dice until **you** have drawn one card from the Community Chest pile.
Avoid:	For the **student** to grasp basic physics, **he** must understand the principles of energy, light, and matter.
Better:	To grasp basic physics, **one** must understand the principles of energy, light, and matter.

4. Reword sentences to eliminate the pronouns or replace them with gender-free words such as *a, an,* and *the.*

   Avoid: Each evening, a **night guard** makes **his** rounds of the building.
   Better: Each evening, a **night guard** patrols **the** building.
   Avoid: The **dietitian** prepares **her** nutritional analysis once a day.
   Better: The **dietitian** prepares **a** nutritional analysis once a day.

5. Use the passive voice occasionally instead of the active voice.

   Active: Whenever an employee enters the building, **he should wear his** identification badge.
   Passive: The identification badge **should be worn** whenever an employee enters the building.

6. To avoid sexist references, repeat the noun if it is separated from the second reference by a number of words.

   Avoid: **The announcer** on a classical music station must know how to pronounce a wide range of foreign names and titles. **He** also must be able to read advertising and news copy.
   Better: **The announcer** on a classical music station must know how to pronounce a wide range of foreign names and titles. **The announcer** also must be able to read advertising and news copy.

Alternative Noun Forms

English has accumulated many nouns that contain the word *man* as a suffix or prefix: *businessman, chairman, congressman, man-hours.* These words can no longer be used to refer to both men and women. The following guidelines give alternatives to these terms.

1. Avoid using *man* to refer to people as a group. Use the terms *humanity, human beings, persons, human race,* or *people* instead.

Avoid: Man (mankind) is at a critical point in his history.

Better: Humanity (the human race) is at a critical point in its history.

Avoid: Man is a gregarious creature.

Better: People are gregarious creatures.

2. Use *person* as the suffix or prefix instead of *man* where the usage would not create absurd constructions (for example, *personhole cover* for *manhole cover*; use *sewer cover* instead).

Avoid: A businessman can fly half fare.

Better: A businessperson can fly half fare.

Avoid: The chairman draws up the agenda.

Better: The chairperson draws up the agenda.

3. Use words other than *person* to replace *man*.

Avoid: The policeman gave me a ticket.

Better: The police officer gave me a ticket.

Avoid: Our mailman came early today.

Better: Our mail carrier came early today.

Avoid: This job will require 24 man-hours.

Better: This job will require 24 staff-hours.

4. Reword the sentence to avoid using *man*.

Avoid: Freshman students are always nervous.

Better: First-year students are always nervous.

Avoid: The team showed unusual gamesmanship.

Better: The team played the game shrewdly.

Suffixes *ess, ette, ix,* and *ienne/ine*

In modern usage, the trend is to drop the suffixes that denote female forms of nouns: *poet, poetess; usher, usherette*. However, three forms are still widely used—*actress, hostess,* and *waitress*. Use the masculine and feminine forms when referring to both men and women.

Incorrect: Alice and Jim served as **hosts.**
Correct: Alice and Jim served as **hostess and host.**

1. Omit the following suffixes, which denote female when added to words.

   ess **Ending**

Avoid	Better
directress	director
authoress	author
sculptress	sculptor

   ette **Ending**

Avoid	Better
usherette	usher
drum majorette	drum major
bachelorette	single

   ix **Ending**

Avoid	Better
aviatrix	aviator
executrix	executor

   ienne/ine **Ending**

Avoid	Better
comedienne	comedian

2. Do not mix gender-inclusive and gender-determined words when pairing men and women.

   Avoid: He is **chairman** of the Elks and she is **chairwoman** of the Junior League. As **chairmen,** they have little time at home.

   Better: He is **chairman** of the Elks, and she is **chairwoman** of the Junior League. As **chairpersons,** they have little time at home.

> **Avoid:** He is **chairperson** of the Elks, and she is **chairwoman** of the Junior League.
>
> **Better:** He is **chairperson** of the Elks, and she is **chairperson** of the Junior League.
>
> He is **chairman** of the Elks, and she is **chairwoman** of the Junior League.

Social Titles

The social titles *Mr.,* *Mrs.,* and *Ms.* can also be used in ways that do not perpetuate stereotypes. Following are some guidelines.

1. Use *Mr.* for all men.

2. Use *Ms.* for all women when you do not know how they prefer to be addressed or do not know their marital status.

3. Use *Miss* or *Mrs.* when the woman herself uses these titles with her name.

4. Use a married woman's first name, not her husband's. For example, use Mrs. Dorothy Brandt, not Mrs. Harold Brandt, unless the woman specifies that she would like to be addressed by her husband's name.

Salutations

In writing business letters or direct mail messages, make sure the salutation includes all the readers who are likely to receive the message. Following are suggested ways to write gender-inclusive salutations.

1. Avoid using *Dear Sir, Dear Gentlemen,* or *My Dear Sirs.* Use the following variations.

   Ladies and Gentlemen:
   Gentlepersons:
   Dear Madames (Mesdames) and Sirs:

My Dear Sirs and Madames (Mesdames):
My Dear Sir or Madam (Madame or Sir):

2. Address individuals by title or group name.

Title	Group Name
Dear Executive:	Dear Customer:
Dear Manager:	Dear Friend:
Dear Human Resources Director:	Dear Subscriber:
Dear Professor:	Dear Investor:
Dear Medical Writer:	To the Folks on Maple:

Occupational Titles

The U.S. Department of Labor in its *Dictionary of Occupational Titles* lists gender-inclusive titles for many occupations and positions. Here are some examples:

Avoid	Revised
salesman	salesperson
craftsman	craftworker
draftsman	drafter
fireman	firefighter
watchman	guard, security officer
newsman	reporter, newsperson
foreman	supervisor
repairman	repairer
mailman	mail carrier, letter carrier
policeman	police, police officer

See the *Dictionary of Occupational Titles* for a complete listing of titles and other business-related terms.

Appendix A

Principal Parts of Irregular Verbs

There are no fixed rules for forming the past tense and past and present participle of irregular verbs. It is necessary to memorize the forms and to keep a good dictionary handy. For reference, some of the most commonly used irregular verbs are listed here.

Basic Form	Past Tense	Past Participle	Present Participle
be	was	been	being
begin	began	begun	beginning
bite	bit	bitten	biting
blow	blew	blown	blowing
break	broke	broken	breaking
bring	brought	brought	bringing
burst	burst	burst	bursting
buy	bought	bought	buying
catch	caught	caught	catching
come	came	come	coming
do	did	done	doing
draw	drew	drawn	drawing
drink	drank	drunk	drinking
drive	drove	driven	driving
eat	ate	eaten	eating
fall	fell	fallen	falling
fight	fought	fought	fighting
flee	fled	fled	fleeing

Basic Form	Past Tense	Past Participle	Present Participle
fly	flew	flown	flying
forget	forgot	forgotten	forgetting
get	got	got/gotten	getting
give	gave	given	giving
go	went	gone	going
grow	grew	grown	growing
hang	hung/hanged	hung/hanged	hanging
hide	hid	hidden	hiding
know	knew	known	knowing
lay	laid	laid	laying
leave	left	left	leaving
lend	lent	lent	lending
lie	lay	lain	lying
lose	lost	lost	losing
pay	paid	paid	paying
ride	rode	ridden	riding
ring	rang	rung	ringing
rise	rose	risen	rising
run	ran	run	running
see	saw	seen	seeing
set	set	set	setting
shake	shook	shaken	shaking
shine	shone	shone	shining
shrink	shrank	shrunk	shrinking
sit	sat	sat	sitting
speak	spoke	spoken	speaking
steal	stole	stolen	stealing
strike	struck	struck	striking
take	took	taken	taking
tear	tore	torn	tearing
throw	threw	thrown	throwing
wear	wore	worn	wearing
write	wrote	written	writing

Appendix B

Verb-Preposition Combinations

Verb-preposition combinations often defy attempts to categorize them under any logical system. As a result, the only solution is to learn through practice which prepositions are used with which verbs under what circumstances. Some of the more troublesome ones are presented here.

agree with, agree to
agree with—concur in opinion (agree with a person)
I **agree with** Carl that we should operate tomorrow.
agree to—give assent (agree to an idea or thing)
I **agree to** an operation for my ulcer.

angry with/at
angry with/at—enraged; *angry at*—suggests a confrontation
She was **angry with** herself for sleeping late.
The president was **angry at** the board for turning down his five-year plan.

answer to, answer for
answer to—be accountable to a person; respond to
You'll have to **answer to** the commission for your sales record.
The dog is four years old and **answers to** the name "Fred."
answer for—be accountable for actions
You'll have to **answer for** your decision to cancel the concert.

on behalf of, in behalf of
on behalf of—as someone's representative
The lawyer acted **on behalf of** my brother to settle the estate.
in behalf of—in someone's interest
I set up a trust fund **in behalf of** my nephew.

belong to, belong with
belong to—be a member of
They **belong to** the Secret Order of the Koala.
belong with—be classified or placed among
These flowers **belong with** the plants classified as grasses.

capacity to, capacity of
capacity to—capable of (used with a verb)
She has the **capacity to** break the world's high-jump record.
capacity of—content or volume (used with a measure)
This silo has a **capacity of** 2,400 cubic feet.

compare to, compare with
compare to—liken
She **compared** my singing **to** Tina Turner's.
"Shall I **compare** thee **to** a summer's day?"
compare with—contrast for similarities and differences
He **compared** the Russian military strength **with** that of the armed
    forces of the United States.

concur in, concur with
concur in—agree (in an opinion)
The three judges **concurred in** their settlement of the case.
concur with—agree (with another person)
I must **concur with** the judge that the settlement is fair.

connect to, connect with
connect to—join (one object to another)
The first step is to **connect** the positive wire **to** the positive pole.
connect with—make contact with (a person, group, idea)
If we drive overnight, we can **connect with** the first group by dawn.

correspond to, correspond with

correspond to—match

The handwriting on this letter **corresponds to** the handwriting on the earlier document.

correspond with—exchange messages

Janet has **corresponded with** a friend in Costa Rica for three years.

differ from, differ with

differ from—be unlike

The movie **differed from** the book in several ways.

differ with—disagree with

The figures in the government report **differ with** those in our study.

inside, inside of

inside (no preposition)—the part lying within

I damaged the **inside** door of our house.

inside of—within (also used with expressions of time)

The flower shop is **inside of** the building.

He will return **inside of** an hour.

in the market, on the market

in the market—looking to buy something

We're **in the market** for a great chocolate dessert.

on the market—up for sale

Hal put his boat **on the market** yesterday and hopes to sell it soon.

name

name (no preposition)—to appoint

Paula was **named** editor in chief of the *Los Angeles Chronicle*. (never "named as" editor in chief)

outside, outside of

outside (no preposition)—the part lying without

I put the poster on the **outside** wall.

outside of—outside; except, other than

She went **outside of** the house.

I can't think of anyone in the office, **outside of** Julio, who knows how to program this computer.

promote, promote to
promote (no preposition)—to increase in rank or status (use with a
    title)
She was **promoted** Lieutenant Commander.
promote to—to raise to a higher rank or status
She was **promoted to** the executive level in the sales department.

reference to, reference on
reference to—a pointing toward
The governor made a **reference to** the health-care legislation, calling
    it "long overdue."
reference on—books or articles about
Tarn's *Babylon* is a scholarly **reference on** the downfall of the Persian
    Empire.

report of/on
report of/on—a written or verbal description (prepositions used
    interchangeably)
He completed a 200-page **report on** why people prefer handheld
    toothbrushes to electric ones.

separate from
separate from (never *separate out*)—to divide; to distinguish
We'll have to **separate** the damaged phones **from** the working ones.
Jerilyn's bank accounts are **separate from** her brother's.

sympathy with, sympathy for
sympathy with—sharing another's feelings
I can **sympathize with** Jack; he has to babysit tonight, and so do I.
sympathy for—having compassion for another
I feel **sympathy for** anyone who has lost a job.

wait for, wait on, wait out
wait for—to be ready or at hand for
The general **waited for** the signal to attack.

wait on—to serve

When my father was in school, he earned money **waiting on** tables.

wait out—colloquial expression meaning to remain inactive during the course of

The fans **waited out** the rainstorm by taking shelter under the bleachers.

write to

write to—send messages to (preposition always used when direct object is missing)

I will **write to** you when you get to Chicago. (Direct object is missing.)

I will **write you** a note when you get to Chicago. (Direct object "note" is present.)

Appendix C

Frequently Confused Words

The meaning and spelling of the following words are commonly confused. Practice using them until the correct usage is familiar to you.

accept, except
accept—to take, agree
I accept the offer.
except—excluding, omitting
Everyone left **except** me.

advice, advise
advice—opinion, counsel
She needs your **advice**.
advise—to counsel
Please **advise** him of his rights.

affect, effect
affect—to influence, change
Inflation always **affects** our level of income.
effect—(n.) impression, results; (v.) to cause
The computer has had a profound **effect** on our everyday lives. It has **effected** a complete change in the way we do business.

already, all ready
already—even now
We **already** have a robot.
all ready—all prepared
They're **all ready** to go.

assent, ascent
assent—(v.) to agree; (n.) permission
Did they **assent** to your request? The entire board gave its **assent** to the project.
ascent—advancement
On the third day, they made their **ascent** to the top of Mount Everest.

capital, capitol
capital—seat of government; wealth
The nation's **capital** braced itself for the holiday weekend.
We need more **capital** to finance our new product line.
capitol—government building
They are putting a new roof on the **capitol**.

cite, site, sight
cite—refer to, state
I **cited** my reasons for disagreeing.
site—location
The **site** for our home is lovely.
sight—scene
The city at dawn is a beautiful **sight.**

cloths, clothes
cloths—pieces of cloth
Use soft **cloths** for polishing your silver.
clothes—wearing apparel
Every spring he buys new **clothes** and throws out the old ones.

complement, compliment
complement—something that completes
Her humor is the perfect **complement** to my seriousness.

compliment—to say something good about someone; a flattering remark

My father always **compliments** my mother on her painting.

The boss's **compliment** meant a lot to Carl.

consul, council, counsel

consul—foreign embassy official

The Swedish **consul** threw a party for the President.

council—official body

The city **council** passed the ordinance by a three-to-one margin.

counsel—(v.) to advise; (n.) legal advisor

Find someone to **counsel** you about your accident. In fact, you should hire the company lawyer to act as **counsel** in this matter.

dissent, descent, descend

dissent—disagreement

Mine was the only vote in **dissent** of the proposed amendment.

descent—a decline, fall

The road made a sharp **descent** and then curved dangerously to the right.

descend—to come down

They had to **descend** from the mountaintop in darkness.

fewer, less

fewer—used for individual units, numbers

You will have to make **fewer** mistakes or order more erasers.

We have five **fewer** doughnuts than we had this morning.

less—used for general quantities

The amount of money in our bank account is **less** than it was last year.

formerly, formally

formerly—previously

I was **formerly** a recruiter.

formally—officially

She was sworn in **formally** as the fifth member of the panel.

imply, infer

imply—to suggest

Are you **implying** that I was at the scene of the crime?

infer—to deduce from evidence

Your gloves were found in the room; thus, we **infer** that you visited the deceased sometime last night.

it's, its

it's—contraction of *it is* or *it has*

It's [it has] been a long day.

I've seen the play; **it's** [it is] not very good.

its—possessive form of the pronoun *it*

When the ship fired **its** guns, the blast was deafening.

later, latter

later—after a time

They'll mail it **later** today.

latter—last mentioned of the two

If it's a choice between the beach and the mountains, I'll take the **latter**.

lead, led, lead

lead—(v.) to go before; (adj.) first

The boys always **lead** the rush to the beach.

The **lead** singer seems off tonight.

led—(v., past tense of *lead*) went before

They **led** the parade playing their kazoos.

lead—(n.) heavy metal; graphite

This paperweight is made of **lead**.

lie, lay

lie—to rest or recline (lie, lay, lain)

The cat always **lies** down on my sweater. Yesterday he **lay** on it all day. I wish he had **lain** somewhere else.

lay—to put or place something (lay, laid, laid)

I will **lay** the sweater on the couch. Yesterday I **laid** it there without thinking about the cat. I have **laid** it there many times.

lose, loose, loss
lose—misplace
Don't **lose** the tickets.
loose—not fastened down; release
The screw is **loose** on the showerhead.
Turn the kids **loose** in the park.
loss—deprivation
His leaving was a **loss** to the company.

past, passed
past—(n., adj.) preceding
The **past** president gave the gavel to the new president.
passed—(v., past tense of *pass*) went by; gone by
We **passed** my cousin on the road.

personal, personnel
personal—individual
Can I ask you a **personal** question?
personnel—a department; workers
The human resources (**personnel**) office keeps records on all
    company **personnel.**

precede, proceed
precede—to come before
My older brother **precedes** me by one grade in school.
proceed—to go ahead
We can **proceed** with our game as soon as the weather clears.

principle, principal
principle—rule, standard
Sound **principles** can help you make good decisions.
principal—(adj.) main, chief; (n.) superintendent
She is the state's **principal** witness in this case.
I'll never forget my grade school **principal**, Mr. Harvey.

quiet, quite

quiet—silent

The valley is **quiet** at dusk.

quite—completely; to a considerable degree

He was **quite** upset with himself for losing the race.

I **quite** agree that the judge was unfair.

rise, raise

rise—(v.) to go up, to get up; (n.) reaction

The moon **rises** later each night.

Your statement to the governor certainly got a **rise** out of him.

raise—(v.) to lift, bring up; (n.) an increase

Raise the picture a little higher.

After four months, he finally got a **raise** in pay.

sit, set

sit—to rest in an upright position

We had to **sit** on the plane for three hours before we took off.

set—to put or place something

They **set** the coffee on the table.

She **set** the files in order.

stationary, stationery

stationary—still, fixed

The chair is **stationary**.

stationery—letter paper

He took out a sheet of **stationery** and wrote a letter.

than, then

than—after a comparison; when

Vivian is taller **than** Kelly.

I no sooner started talking **than** Kelly interrupted me.

then—next; in that case

She took Fred's order and **then** mine.

If you want to skip the mashed potatoes, **then** have the waitress mark
  it on the order.

that, which
that—used to introduce a phrase or clause essential to the meaning of
the sentence; not set off by commas
The shipment **that** arrived yesterday had to be returned. (*That arrived
yesterday* identifies which shipment had to be returned and is
essential information.)
We ate the 15 doughnuts **that** Jan brought to work this morning.
which—used to refer to a specific noun or pronoun and to introduce a
phrase or clause not essential to the meaning of the sentence;
usually set off by commas
We ate 15 doughnuts, **which** was 15 too many. (*Which* refers to
doughnuts and adds additional information—*which was 15 too
many*—that is not essential to the meaning of the sentence.)
The shipment, **which** arrived yesterday, had to be returned. (*Which
arrived yesterday* is incidental information and is set off by
commas.)

Exception: that or *which* can at times be used interchangeably to avoid
too many repetitions of either word in a sentence.

there, their, they're
there—a place
The book has to be on the table; I saw it **there** just a minute ago.
their—possessive form of *they*
Why don't they take **their** skateboards and go home?
they're—contraction of *they are*
They're upset that the watermelon fell off the table.

weather, whether
weather—climate
The **weather** has been changing slowly over the past fifty years.
whether—if; regardless
They have to know **whether** you are going. You should tell them
whether you feel like it or not.

who's, whose

who's—contraction of *who is* or *who has*

Do you know **who's** [who is] coming to the party tonight? No, I don't know **who's** [who has] been invited.

whose—possessive form of *who*

Whose purple car is parked outside our house?

you're, your

you're—contraction of *you are*

You're going to be late for dinner.

your—possessive form of *you*

Your dinner is cold.

Appendix D

Frequently Misspelled Words

The following list contains words that are frequently misspelled. Use this list as a quick reference in addition to consulting a good dictionary.

abbreviate
absence
abundant
accessible
accidentally
accommodate
accompanies
accompaniment
accumulate
accuracy
acknowledgment
acquaintance
adequately
admission
admittance
adolescent
advantageous
allege
alliance
analysis
analyze
anonymous
apologetically
apparatus
apparent

appreciate
appropriate
argument
arrangement
arrears
ascertain
association
attendance
authorize
auxiliary
awfully

ballet
bankruptcy
beneficial
bibliography
bookkeeper
boulevard
brochure
buffet
bulletin

calculation
calendar
camouflage

canceled/cancelled
cancellation
catalog/catalogue
catastrophe
category
cellar
cemetery
changeable
choose
chose
colossal
column
commitment
committed
committee
comparative
competent
competition
competitor
complexion
comptroller
conceivable
concise
conscience
conscientious
consciousness
consensus
consistency
contingency
controlling
controversy
correspondence
correspondents
criticize
curriculum

debacle
debtor
decadent
deceitful
deference
deferred

dependent
depreciation
description
desirable
detrimental
dilemma
diligence
disastrous
disciple
discrimination
dissatisfied
division

economical
ecstasy
effect
efficiency
embarrassment
emphasize
endeavor
enforceable
enormous
enthusiastically
entrance
espionage
exaggerate
excel
exceptionally
exhaustion
exhibition
exhibitor
exhilaration
existence
exorbitant
expensive
extension
exuberant

facilitate
familiar
familiarize
fascination

feasible
feminine
financier
foreign
forfeit
franchise
fraud
fraudulent
freight
fulfill

gauge
grammar
grievance
guarantee
guaranty
guidance

harassment
hereditary
hindrance
horizontal
hygiene
hypocrisy
hypothetical

ideally
idiomatic
illegible
immediately
imperative
implement
incidentally
inconvenience
indemnity
independent
indispensable
inevitable
inflationary
influential
ingenious
initial

initiative
innocent
inoculate
institution
intellectual
interference
interpretation
interrupt
invoice
irrelevant
irresistible
itemize
itinerary

jeopardize
jeopardy
judgment/judgement

kerosene
knowledge
knowledgeable

labeled
laborious
larynx
legitimate
leisurely
liable
license
likelihood
livelihood
liquor
livable
loose
lose
lucrative
luxurious

magistrate
magnificence
maintenance
majestic

malicious
manageable
mandatory
maneuver
marketable
marriageable
martyrdom
materialism
measurable
mediator
mediocre
melancholy
metaphor
miniature
miscellaneous
mischievous
misspell
misstatement
mortgage
mosquito
municipal
mysterious

naive
necessity
negligible
negotiate
neurotic
neutral
ninety
ninth
noticeable

objectionable
observant
occasionally
occupant
occurrence
omission
omitting
opinionated
opportunity

option
outrageous
overrated

pageant
pamphlet
parallel
paralysis
parity
parliament
particularly
pastime
pedestal
penicillin
permanent
permissible
permitted
persistent
personal
perspiration
phenomenon
physician
picnicking
plausible
pneumonia
politician
possession
practically
precede
precise
preference
preferred
prejudice
presence
prestige
presumption
prevalent
privilege
procedure
propaganda
prophesy
prove

psychoanalysis
psychology
pursue

qualitative
quality
quantitative
quantity
questionnaire
quietly
quit
quite

rebellion
receive
recommend
recommendation
reconciliation
recurrence
reducible
reference
referred
rehearsal
reimburse
relieve
reminiscent
remittance
remitted
repetition
representative
resource
respectfully
responsibility
returnable
reveal
revenue
routine

salable/saleable
schedule
scientific
scrutinize

separation
sergeant
serviceable
siege
significant
similar
souvenir
specifically
specimen
sponsor
statistics
strategic
stubbornness
substantial
succeed
succession
superficial
superfluous
superintendent
supersede
supervisor
suppress
surroundings
susceptible
symbolic
symmetrical
synonymous

tariff
technician
temperature
tendency
theoretical
tolerance
tomorrow
traffic
tragedy
transcend
transmit
transmittal
transparent
tried

twelfth
tyranny

unanimous
undoubtedly
uniform
universal
unmistakable
unnatural
unnecessary
unscrupulous

vaccine
vacuum
variation
vehicle
vengeance
ventilation
versatile
vigilance

villain
vinegar
volume

waive
warranty
welcome
whisper
whistle
wholly
withhold

yacht
yawn
yield
young
youth

zealous
zenith

Glossary

Active voice: the subject of a sentence performs an action (I *delivered* the book.)

Adjective: word used to modify a noun, pronoun, or another adjective; answers the questions *What kind? How many? Which one? How much?*

Adverb: word that modifies a verb, adjective, or another adverb; answers the questions *When? Where? How much? In what manner?*

Antecedent: the word or words in a sentence to which a pronoun refers

Apostrophe: punctuation mark used to show possession, to form contractions, and to form the plural of many nouns and symbols (several *8's* in this sentence)

Auxiliary verb: a verb such as *has, am, were* used with a past or present participle to signal a change in verb tense or form (he walks; he *is walking*) or a change in voice (we told; we *were told*); also known as a helping verb

Brackets: a pair of punctuation marks used to enclose additions to quoted material or additions to material already enclosed in parentheses

Buzzwords: terms that come into fashion for a time, usually borrowed from various professions and adapted to general use (dicey, rip-off)

Case: the nominative, objective, and possessive forms of a personal pronoun (they, them, theirs)

Clause: a group of words that contain a subject-verb combination; independent clauses express a complete thought (he lifted the box), while subordinate clauses are incomplete thoughts (while he lifted the box)

Cliché: any trite, worn-out expression that should be avoided in writing (cold as ice)

Collective noun: a word that refers to a group of people, animals, objects, or other units (family)

Colon: a punctuation mark used to represent a more complete stop than a semicolon but not as complete a stop as a period; also used with the direct address in formal correspondence

Comma: a punctuation mark used to separate words or groups of words in a list or parallel construction, to separate elements in a sentence, or to punctuate direct address

Common noun: a word that refers to a general category and is not capitalized (machine)

Comparative form: adding the suffix *er* or the word *more* to show the difference between persons, places, or things (taller, more quietly)

Comparisons: adjectives and adverbs used to show degrees of difference among persons, places, or things; the forms are positive (tall, quietly), comparative (taller, more quietly), and superlative (tallest, most quietly)

Complete subject: a noun or pronoun and all its modifiers that serve as the topic of a sentence (*The rotting old willow* finally split in two.)

Complex sentence: a sentence that contains an independent clause and one or more subordinate clauses (*While giving her speech*, [subordinate clause] she knocked over the microphone.)

Compound adjective: two adjectives used to modify a noun (a lens with a *wide angle*); if they precede the noun, they are usually hyphenated (*wide-angle* lens)

Compound-complex sentence: a sentence that contains two or more independent clauses and one or more subordinate clauses (She's not coming, and I don't know why *even though we're friends.* [subordinate clause])

Compound predicate: two or more verbs, objects, or complements that are joined by a coordinating conjunction (The runner *started out in front but finished last.*)

Compound sentence: a sentence that contains two or more independent clauses but no subordinate clauses (She's not coming, and I don't know why.)

Compound subject: two subjects joined by *and, or,* or *nor* (*Pete and Vinnie* drove home.)

Conditional form: a verb phrase that uses *may, can, will,* or *shall* plus another verb to express intention to do or be something (I *could see* it if I had my glasses on; I *should get* them.); the conditional form can be used with all six tenses

Conjunction: links words or groups of words to other parts of a sentence and shows the relationship between them; four types of conjunctions: coordinating, correlative, and subordinating, plus linking adverbs

Coordinating conjunction: a word such as *and, but, or,* or *nor* that joins two or more elements of equal rank in a sentence (love and hate)

Correlative conjunction: coordinating conjunctions used in pairs, such as *both-and, either-or,* and *neither-nor* that join two or more elements of equal rank in a sentence and emphasize the elements being joined (*neither* fish *nor* fowl)

Dangling modifiers: descriptive phrases or clauses joined to the wrong words in a sentence (*Holding hands, our dogs* went with us as we walked to the park.)

Dash: a punctuation mark longer than a hyphen used to indicate a break in thought or the addition of information

Declarative sentence: a sentence that makes a statement or asks a question

Definite article: limiting adjective *the* that refers to one or more specific items

Demonstrative adjective: a word such as *which, what, this, these, that,* or *those* used to emphasize which items are being singled out and their distance from the speaker (He gave us two boxes. *This one* is mine.)

Demonstrative pronoun: a pronoun such as *here* or *there* used to indicate nearness or distance from the speaker (He gave us two boxes. Mine is over *here.*)

Direct object: a word, phrase, or clause that receives the action of the verb (They mailed the *package.*)

Ellipses: a series of three periods used to indicate that material has been left out from a quotation or quoted material

Exclamation point: an end mark used to express strong emotion or to catch the reader's attention

Fragment: a phrase or clause that does not express a complete thought and is missing either a subject or a verb (the shuttle on the launchpad—*no verb*)

Future perfect tense: a verb form used to express an action, state of being, or condition that will be completed in the future (I *will have seen* the movie by then.)

Future tense: a verb form used to express an action, state of being, or condition that will occur in the future (I *will see* it soon.)

Gender: the masculine or feminine forms of a noun (chairman, chairwoman) or a pronoun (he, she)

Gender-inclusive language: words and phrases used to create gender-neutral terms (fireman = firefighter) and to avoid reinforcing stereotypes of men and women in written work

Gerund: a verb form ending in *ing* that is used as a noun (*Hiking* is great exercise.)

Hyphen: a punctuation mark used to join two or more words, names, or numbers that are used as a single unit; to join some prefixes and suffixes to their nouns; and to divide words into syllables

Imperative mood: used for commands or requests, usually with the subject *you* understood (*Give* me that pencil. *Ron, please hand* me that pencil.)

Indefinite article: limiting adjectives *a* and *an* that refer to an unspecified item

Indefinite pronoun: a pronoun such as *all, any,* or *some* that refers to unspecified people or things (*Any* clue will do.)

Independent clause: a group of words that contains a subject-verb combination and expresses a complete thought (I gave at the office.)

Indicative mood: used when the speaker or writer wishes to make a statement or ask a question

Indirect object: a word or group of words that receives the action of the subject (Carl gave *him* the medals.)

Infinitive: verb form used with the preposition *to* (to think)

Infinitive phrase: a phrase that includes an infinitive and is used as a noun (*To play with others* is a child's way of learning about the world.)

Interjection: a word used to express strong emotion or to catch the reader's attention

Interrogative pronoun: a pronoun such as *who, whom, whose, what,* or *which* used to introduce a question (*What* was I thinking?)

Irregular verb: a verb whose base form changes to form the past participle and/or past tense (draw, drew, drawn)

Italics: a special form of type used to indicate emphasis; the names of ships, spacecraft, and other major vehicles; foreign terms and phrases not commonly used; and the titles of novels, plays, movies, operas, and other major works

Jargon: specialized terms of a profession that the general reader probably doesn't understand

Limiting adjective: a word used to identify or number the noun it modifies (*few* apples)

Linking adverb: an adverb used to join two independent clauses and to show the relationship between the clauses (We didn't like the show; *however,* we loved the music.)

Modifier: any word or group of words used to limit, qualify, or add information to the meaning of other words or other parts of a sentence

Mood: using a verb to express differences in the intention of the speaker or writer; three moods in English: indicative, imperative, and subjunctive

Nonrestrictive clause: a clause that adds additional information about a person, place, or object but is not essential to the meaning of the sentence; set off by commas from the rest of the sentence (The soup, *which is really spicy,* is a good appetizer.)

Noun: a word that refers to a person, place, or thing (wisdom)

Number: the singular or plural form of a noun, pronoun, or verb (car, cars; his, theirs; she drives, we drive)

Parentheses: a pair of punctuation marks used to enclose material that is an interruption of the text but adds information

Passive voice: the subject of a sentence receives the action (I *was given* a book.)

Past participle: a verb form made by adding *ed* to the base of a regular verb (laugh, laughed) or by using the special form of an irregular verb (do, done); used in verb phrases (I *have done* nothing for several days.)

Past perfect tense: a verb form used to express an action, state of being, or condition that was completed in the past before another past action or event (I *had seen* it twice before it *disappeared.*)

Past tense: verb form used to indicate actions or states of being or conditions that have been completed in the past (I *watched* it.); formed by adding *ed* to the base form or by using the special form of an irregular verb (It *went* away.)

Period: an end mark used at the end of a complete sentence, which can be a statement, command, or request

Person: the pronoun form used to indicate the speaker (I, we), the person the speaker addresses (you), or the person or thing about whom the speaker is talking (he/him, she/her, it/they)

Personal pronoun: a word that takes the place of a noun and can express person, case, and gender (Glenda is a good witch, but *she* has an evil sister.)

Phrasal preposition: a preposition that consists of more than one word (because of, in spite of)

Phrase: group of related words that do not contain a subject-verb combination (on the sidewalk, going down the ramp)

Positive form of comparison: the base adjective or adverb used to indicate a degree or quality of something in a person, place, or thing (That boy is *tall.*)

Possessive noun: a word used to indicate ownership or relationship (company's stock)

Predicate: a group of words that includes the verb and describes or explains the subject of a sentence (The first train *came around the bend much too fast.*)

Predicate adjective: adjective that follows a linking verb such as *feel, become, seem, get, is, look,* or *smell* that refers to the condition of the subject (He looks *pale.*)

Prefix: a word part added to the beginning of a word that changes the word's meaning (*pre* + heat = preheat)

Preposition: connecting word that shows the relationship among words in a sentence

Prepositional phrase: a preposition plus the nouns, pronouns, gerund phrases, or noun clauses used as an adjective or adverb (That ball *on the floor* is glowing; set it *on the counter.*)

Present participle: a verb form made by adding *ing* to the base of a verb (do, doing); used in verb phrases (I *am doing* nothing right now.)

Present perfect tense: a verb form used to express an action, state of being, or condition occurring at an indefinite time in the past or that continues to the present (I *have seen* it many times now.)

Present tense: a verb used to express an action, state of being, or condition that occurs at the present time (I *see* it.)

Progressive form: a verb form that emphasizes the continuity of an action, state of being, or condition rather than its completion (I *am seeing* it right now.); progressive forms can be used with all six tenses

Pronoun: a word that takes the place of a noun or group of words acting as a noun (*The garbage truck* always arrives early. I never hear *it.*)

Proper noun: a capitalized word that refers to a specific person, place, or thing (John Wayne)

Question mark: an end mark used with a sentence that asks a direct question

Quotation marks: used to indicate the titles of poems, short stories, and musical pieces and to indicate someone's exact words

Regular verb: a verb that keeps the same base regardless of changes in form or tense (work, working, worked, have been working, will work)

Relative pronoun: a pronoun such as *who, whom,* or *whose* that can be used to avoid repeating the noun

Restrictive clause: a clause that adds additional information about a person, place, or object and is essential to the meaning of the sentence; not set off by commas (The menu *that we use on weekends* has no breakfast items.)

Run-on sentence: two or more complete thoughts strung together without punctuation (The shuttle is lifting off I'm getting great pictures.)

Semicolon: a punctuation mark that represents a stronger break than a comma but not as complete a stop as a period or colon

Sentence: a group of words that begins with a capital letter, closes with an end mark, and expresses a complete thought (The shuttle will launch tomorrow.)

Simple sentence: an independent clause with no subordinate clauses; begins with a capital letter and ends with an end mark

Simple subject: a noun or pronoun that serves as the topic of a sentence (The young *conductor* is changing the sound of the orchestra.)

Subject: a noun, pronoun, phrase, or clause that is the topic of the sentence

Subject-verb agreement: a subject and its verb must agree in person and number (*We are* leaving; *he is* staying.)

Subjunctive mood: used with a different form of the present and past tense of a verb to express matters of urgency, formality, possibility, or speculation (If I *were* [not *was*] queen of the universe, things would be different.)

Subordinate clause: a group of words with a subject-verb combination that is not a complete thought (When dinosaurs traveled in herds . . .)

Subordinating conjunction: a word such as *how, although,* or *until* that joins elements of unequal rank in a sentence (We played indoors *until* the rain stopped and the sun came out.)

Suffix: a word part added to the end of a word that changes that word's meaning (break + *able* = breakable)

Superlative form of comparison: adding the suffix *est* or the word *most* to show the differences between or among persons, places, or things (tallest, most quietly)

Tense: forms of verbs used to indicate whether an action or state of being occurs in the past, present, or future (was, is, will be)

Verb: a word or group of words used to express an action, a state of being, or a condition

Verb complement: a word or group of words used to complete the meaning of a sentence containing a linking verb. (They seem *unhappy about the movie's ending.*)

Index